Not One Drop of Blood

6-19-10

Not One Drop of Blood

The Human Side of Prison Versus Probation

John P. Heffernan

Published by
Gray Dog Press
Spokane, Washington
www.GrayDogPress.com

Not One Drop of Blood

For information contact:
Gray Dog Press, 2727 S. MT. Vernon #4
Spokane, Washington 99223

Edited by: Andrew N. Corder

ISBN: 978-1-936178-01-8

Dedication

To Kathy, for without her nothing is possible.

To my co-workers who believed, worked,
and left their footprints in the sand.

To all those offenders who made
bad choices, you made my career.

Acknowledgements

The following persons read my manuscript and contributed constructive criticism. Their help was essential to producing this story.

Robert Lizee
Bob and Barbara Enright
Bob Banta
John Ely
Holly Doering
Art McGinn
Janet Parks
Sr. Esther Heffernan O. P.
John J. Prideaux
James Heffernan
Dwayne Arkills
Mary Farrell
Robert Pillsbury
Andrew N. Corder

Foreword

I write to say there are better ways to deter crime than building prisons. Prisons are not generally effective in encouraging positive behavior and often are fear factories.

I supervised probationers and parolees who were no great risk to citizens; I include some of their names. I began in a simple era knowing little, but I managed and I learned. I engaged offenders and their collateral resources, if successful. I saw that most offenders wanted to stay out of trouble.

I turned down a work release job in April 1971 but accepted a work release supervisor position in the fall when Jerry Savland quit for health reasons. I accepted work release in order to keep self-screening and volunteers in the jail and to integrate both into work release. I stopped direct case supervision in 1971. After work release, I went on to the corrections centers at Geiger in 1979, Pine Lodge in 1983, and Airway Heights in 1991.

As a manager, I kept my goals simple, which empowered both staff and offenders. My first objective was inmate safety. If inmates feel safe, they can change by making positive choices.

In 1967, probation and parole field staffers were transferred to the Department of Institutions. I had no clue that over time the transfer would kill off probation work. Prison and institutional folk were not bad people, but their focus was on prison operations.

The Department of Social and Health Services regionalized operations in 1971, which caused confusion. Public safety suffered and prisons boiled. The Department of Corrections inherited a weak probation effort in 1981 and needed more prison beds. In response, citizens supported the Sentencing Reform Act in 1981, which changed felony sentencing.

But the Sentencing Reform Act ignored the fact that 72 percent of all crimes remained unsolved, and put emphasis on punishment rather than rehabilitation as probation and parole had emphasized. National crime rates grew and values sagged, yet no one looked for a cause, and the trend continued as more young adults went to prison.

Prison must not be a first resort; rather we must look to our communities, families, and schools, as doing so is cheaper and more effective. I say build community resources instead of prisons—it is a much better use of state correctional dollars.

John Heffernan

Contents

The Territorial Prison at Seatco, 1875

Wenatchee
1963–1964

I was born March 17, 1938, to William and Cecilia Heffernan. We were a ranching family in Williston, North Dakota. My first school had one teacher. In 1946, we moved to Willow City, North Dakota and then to St. Ignatius, Montana in 1947.

In 1949 we settled in Spokane, Washington, yet Dad was restless for ranching, so we spent one summer in Montana. I started at Gonzaga High School in 1952. After graduating in 1956, I joined the air force and went through engine school at Sheppard Air Force Base. My first duty was at Shaw AFB in Sumter, South Carolina. In 1958, I had temporary duty at Fairchild AFB near Spokane, and then at Clark AFB in the Philippines. I spent Christmas 1958 on Wake Island.

I had orders to Iceland in July 1959 and I felt unlucky. Yet by March 1960, I had earned eighteen college credits for Gonzaga University. Senator Henry M. Jackson ensured I was discharged on time after a leave in Scotland.

I graduated from Gonzaga University in July 1963 with a BA in physiology. In my last semester I took an exchange student to a criminal justice workshop at Washington State University, which until 1959 had been called Washington State College. It was a bust for him, but there I saw applications for the Washington State Board of Prison Terms and Paroles. On a whim, I filled out the paperwork.

* * *

In September 1963, John Prideaux drove Herb Roll and I to Olympia. We were candidates for jobs in probation and parole. John was a hunter who trained bird dogs, and along the way he pointed out migrating birds. I hoped he would speak of our upcoming interview, but instead he talked hunting and dogs.

In Olympia, at midday, the capitol campus was impressive. The parole board offices were in the Institutions Building, on a floor filled with cabinets and desks. We took a seat between cabinets. Herb interviewed first.

The staff was friendly but businesslike as I waited for my turn, which was not long. Herb walked up slowly. His face was blank.

The interview was the final step. I had taken a written test at the employment office and an oral exam at the courthouse. My mouth was dry as I walked through the oversize walnut doors.

Beyond the doors was a high-ceilinged room with an oak table. I felt tense. Two gray-haired men—one black, the other white—and a woman sat at the table.

The woman smiled and said, "Hello. Please, relax."

She looked at the white man to her right, who said, "I'm George Parks."

To her left the black man said, "I'm Russell Gideon."

Charlotte Groshell introduced herself and said, "Welcome. Did you have a good trip?"

She did not wait for my reply. She stated the parole board's mission, and said, "Please tell us about you."

Mr. Gideon was a retired pharmacist who had been in World War II, and he was impressed by my military service. Mr. Parks asked me about Spokane's political leaders.

"Do you know Joe Smith?" he asked.

I had expected technical or legal questions, to which I would have replied, "I know little about probation and parole work."

Gideon's head nodded. His chin was on his chest. I thought, "Oh God! Gideon is asleep!" Thrown off, I replied to Parks.

"No, I don't know Mr. Smith, but I've heard his name."

Parks then asked, "If the board policies say do this, but your boss said do the opposite, what will you do?"

I was glad I hadn't quit my bank job yet. I felt he was judging my integrity, so I gave a basic military reply.

"I would follow the boss's orders, as he has your support."

Suddenly, the tension in the room broke. Parks darkened and Gideon awoke.

Groshell smiled and said, "Thank you." She looked to Gideon, who nodded.

Groshell turned to me and said, "You did fine. You're hired."

Parks left without shaking my hand. Groshell told me I was her last interview; she had a federal parole job in California. "Good luck," she said.

Gideon shook my hand and wished me luck.

That was it. My interview was over. I carried my news and my grin down the hall. Herb had also been hired.

We spent the night in Seattle near the Space Needle. Prideaux bought dinner. Herb was to start his job in Spokane. My post was Wenatchee. It would be a $45 per month raise over my bank job.

Ducks hid in the cornfields on the trip home. I could not believe that on a whim at a criminal justice workshop, with no planning, I had gained a career.

Left to Right: Charlotte Paul Groshell, H. J. Lawrence, Harris G. Hunter, Russell S. Gideon, and George F. Parks

* * *

Citizens link illegal acts to immorality. Yet laws are legal codes, not biblical edicts, and legal systems are process driven. For an action to be illegal, a law has to say the act is illegal. Removing morality from the equation is a change in thinking.

I made my living off crime. No crime meant no crooks, and no work for parole board employees. My job was to work myself out of a job; that was not likely.

People may be surprised to learn that a good economy also grows the rate of crime; the social structure weakens in a growth culture. With economic growth, crime rates soared in step with population. In 1963, the state of Washington had 6,707 adult offenders—2,577 in prisons and 4,130 on supervision. A new corrections center opened in 1964, and a women's prison opened at Gig Harbor in 1968.

America at the time was an industrial engine, and gas was cheap. Growth was rags to riches and rapid. We moved past previous limits to fortune and glory. Mobility meant the kind of freedom that allows for new beginnings. Fads arrived, industries grew, and we placed a man on the moon.

Technology supplanted discipline in education. Moms were part time at home, full time at work. Children baby-sat by TV grew vacant and self-centered. People spent more time with Ozzie and Harriet than with their families. Conflict was on television nightly.

Nationally, an era of civil rights developed, but in the South, the justice system and families supported the status quo, so folks were denied their constitutional and civil rights a hundred years after the Civil War. Values were a barrier as rights collided with southern institutions. The unintended consequences weakened families and schools as life turned upside down.

Southern police defended segregation with fire hoses in the streets and with words in courts. A protest was civil disobedience!

In the West we were less aware still, as segregation shaded us. Social reforms were like earthquakes with aftershocks that destroyed the social landscape. Changing laws is easy; changing hearts is difficult.

* * *

Before I was hired, I knew little of Olympia, which in 1940 had been a sleepy town. When Governor Arthur Langlie took office in 1941, Olympia's influence in Washington State grew. Langlie served two more terms from 1949–1957 and was followed by Al Rosellini, who built on his efforts.

When Rosellini took office, the chairman of the Washington State Board of Prison Terms and Paroles was Dr. Henry Ness, of the Sociology Department at the University of Washington. His parole board staff of twenty-nine officers was in courthouses around the state. Ness hired Vincent O'Leary, one of his graduate students, as chief parole and probation officer.

O'Leary then hired master's program graduates Robert Austin and Ellis Stout. The rest of his staff was ex-police, grandfathered in. James Skaggs, the next board chair after Ness, sought professionalism and promoted Robert Austin to O'Leary's post. In 1955 the Division of Probation and Parole moved its office from the City-County Building in Seattle to the Institutions Building in Olympia with the parole board's office. In 1958 the board was expanded to five members. Forty-seven staff members worked statewide during that time of growth.

Austin was blunt and hotheaded, and wanted to remove staff from the board, which had become political. He pushed hard, but Governor Rosellini vetoed the effort even after staffers lobbied him to make the change. Staffers and the public did not forget Rosellini's veto.

Austin quit in 1962 after arguments with new chairman Harris Hunter. Ellis Stout was named acting chief.

Also in 1962, talks started for the transfer of the parole board to the Department of Institutions as a merger of field and prison staff. The eastern area manager, Bob Lizee, supported the merger effort.

I met Bob Lizee after returning from my interview in Olympia. Bob had grown up in Yakima and attended Marquette High School.

He had played on Yakima's state championship legion baseball team, then played semi-pro ball before joining the Army Air Corp in World War II. He flew as a belly gunner over England and was shot down twice. He was willing to fly in heavy flak.

Bob had met his wife, Dotty, at Gonzaga University, where he attended on the GI Bill. After graduation, he taught at Reardan High School before working at the local welfare office. He hired on to the parole board in 1951. He was eventually elevated to eastern area supervisor. Bob flared at the mention of Harris Hunter or Governor Rosellini. He did not consider politics a proper subject in probation and parole work.

John Prideaux, Bob's deputy, was the one who had taken Herb Roll and I to our interviews. John had grown up in Everett, Washington, and was a Washington State College graduate. He served a tour in Korea as a first lieutenant with the military police. Later he had been hired at the Vancouver, Washington, parole office.

John had married his wife, Ann, in Walla Walla after moving there to replace a staffer named Wood, who had died. John later declined a promotion to area supervisor in the Seattle office because Ann worked for the superior court in Spokane.

* * *

Wenatchee was the apple capital of the world as I started work on October 8, 1963. The town sat on the Columbia River among bare hills hiding apple orchards in the valleys. Our offices were in a building at Mission and Second Street.

John Prideaux introduced me to Dave Schafer and Bob Reeder in Wenatchee. Dave, the lead officer, supervised Chelan County cases. Bob worked Grant County in the Columbia basin. My cases would be in Okanogan, Ferry, and Douglas counties.

With Dave's help, I found an apartment on Second Street. Wenatchee was home to Dave and his wife Helen. Tall and lanky, Dave covered ground quickly.

Dave was easygoing and polite, and was never in public work hours without a tie and a dark suit. He wore glasses to read, his head seemed too small, and he had thinning brown hair. He also liked to bet on the ponies.

Dave had been an orphan, taken in—but never adopted—by an elderly couple, who left him their estate. He had served in Brazil in World War II in the Army Air Corp. Upon returning, he had hired on as a sheriff deputy, and was a political appointee to probation and parole.

Bob Reeder was a Utah native. The first time we met, he said, "I'm Mormon, Dave's nothing. What are you?"

I said, "I'm Catholic."

"Good," Bob said.

Reeder managed his church's local welfare programs. Bob and his wife had young children and lived in east Wenatchee. He drank no coffee or alcohol, only Pepsi.

His clothes were off Salvation Army store racks and matched his shaggy hair. He was short and pugnacious and had a photographic memory, which he hid with a dry humor. When his eyes darted about, I knew a story or a joke was coming. He and Schafer got on well, but Bob's one-liners on some days were too much for Dave.

* * *

I had no clue as to what to expect from my new job. I tagged along or sat in on meetings. Stories or anecdotes at coffee provided some background, yet I was not streetwise. I lacked context. I was in the game yet I knew I did not know much. I hoped that Dave or Bob would give me the inside scoop. Instead, I got a fifty-page book of report examples. There was no summary of policy or philosophy, just report examples. I asked questions and was answered with questions. The lack of direction was frustrating.

Dave asked me about school, friends, military life, and career plans. He praised me as being overqualified for the "off-the-wall" job I'd gotten.

"Familiarize yourself with your cases, and then we can talk. If you want, join me when I have visitors," was Dave's sole direction.

During my first days, Dave introduced me to local officials. He was well known, and I felt welcome but out of place.

We started in the Apple Café at 8 a.m., at a table beyond the back booths. People nodded as we entered. There was coffee and talk as plans were made and shared. I sat quietly, listening for wisdom. But talk was of events, cases, or rumors from Olympia; I got no road map.

Throughout those weeks, my days were spent reading files and reports. My caseload was seventy cases, which sat in a cabinet. Some files were slim, others thick, each a story or ongoing dialogue. It was easy to get lost in those files. They were logs of case activity, and there were variations in writing skills and viewpoints depending on the authors.

One writer wrote acronyms, the shorthand of the pros in the business. Others wrote plain English. Each review brought up more questions, so I read them again, and then did a third review. I tried to connect the dots. My job was to impact outcomes, and I was worried about public safety. I hoped to do the right thing and not risk big mistakes.

I felt wrung out at day's end.

* * *

One morning at the café, Dave said, "Tomorrow we travel up to Okanogan, Ferry, and Douglas counties. You will meet the officials up north."

We had eight hours together on the trip upriver. Apple season was in full swing, so the country was alive. Dave drove and talked, and I wrote down everything. Dave knew sheriffs' deputies, town marshals, and court clerks, including Sheriff George Wills and Judge Murray. I scribbled notes lest I forget a comment.

I was so busy that I ignored the beauty of the Columbia River, as migrating geese hugged its banks for safety. No hunting was allowed on the river and the birds seemed to know it.

Late in the afternoon, we stopped at Dave's cabin at Lake Chelan, a beautiful quiet spot. His cabin sat among trees on the lake, and I saw why Dave liked his life.

I was inspired and impressed by my trip with Dave, so it was with energy that I pored over my faceless files, asking, "What is vital?"

I wanted cookbook answers, but my career was not going to be gift-wrapped for me—I had to experience, work, and practice. I had no formulas to study and no simple answers.

I memorized what I could. Pink reports were for violations, salmon-colored ones were requests for investigation, pale blue or white were progress reports. I looked for word patterns. I read incomplete stories of which I was now a part.

But reading a fitness book does not make you fit. Fitness is a goal that requires effort, energy, and work. It was months before I realized my learning curve would be a five-year journey full of trial and error. On a people-to-people stage you never get to a point where you stop learning; every case is unique.

* * *

My first solo trip was to do pre-parole investigations on my caseload and verify that clients were following their stated plans. The people in my cases were still a mystery. My territory started with one case in Manson, a village on Lake Chelan's north shore. I traveled north to Omak, Brewster, Twisp, and Tonasket, then on to Oroville—a grand tour. Deer roamed in fields near farmhouses, and Methow Valley was a wonder that time of year as the trees turned copper and gold.

The valley had no street addresses and I circled to find a parole sponsor. In Twisp, I met a town marshal who helped me locate her. The case sponsor's son was welcoming and told me that a logger had work for Bill, the parolee. The logger's wife confirmed Bill's job.

My file said Bill drank, and I counted five taverns in Twisp. The marshal said he would call me if he saw Bill drinking.

Bill's mother lived alone and was looking forward to his return. I felt uneasy asking the middle-aged woman questions. I said that she could help her son by calling me if he drank. I suggested that because loggers worked high-risk jobs, they might drink to let off steam.

* * *

The Loup Loup road went from Twisp to Omak. It was dark as I pulled up to the Caribou Inn Hotel. Luckily they had a room, a café, and a bar. After dinner, I visited a second local sponsor. He had a tavern and card room. He was going to hire a parolee named Charley as a card dealer and pay him with room and board.

The next day I asked Okanogan County Sheriff Wills, "Are card rooms illegal?"

"No," he said. "Omak tolerates gaming, so the plan is okay."

Wills was a rawboned cowboy, but friendly. Before I even sat down, he asked me to speak to the Okanogan County Cattlemen's Association.

"You can talk about what you do, being new to Okanogan," he said.

Caught off guard, it sounded great. He thought I was important and I gave it no thought.

"Yes I will," I said.

After coffee, I drove Highway 97 north to Oroville, and it hit me: What would I say? I might have begged off, but now I was stuck. "Why me?" I wondered. My thoughts bounced about in my head as I arrived in Oroville.

Oroville was the last town on Highway 97 before crossing into Canada near Lake Osoyoos. I had lunch with a town marshal and resident deputy sheriff. Dave and I had not traveled to Oroville, so I was now able to put faces to names of the officials.

After lunch, I traveled back to Tonasket and turned east on Highway 20 toward Republic. It was early afternoon, and sun hit the autumn colors as I drove through a forest. In weeks, snow would cover those woods.

I thought, "This is God's country." In Republic, using Dave's directions, I found Sheriff Daly at his ranch. He was on his tractor cutting hay. He looked more like a farmer than a sheriff. We shook hands and he told me that Jones, a parolee, was not working and was spending time in taverns.

"I should talk to him," he said. "He might need arresting." Daly sounded firm, so I decided to visit Jones.

I got lost twice before I found him. It was late, so I was irritated and in a black mood.

Bluntly, I told Jones, "I'll be back in a week. If you're not working and staying out of the bars, it's jail."

I had forgotten he was my first interview. I was not even nervous.

Jones was unkempt and under-weight, with bad teeth. He was a sad sight in his dirty old jeans—a sad looking man.

He did not react. What would I have done had Jones argued? Later, I looked at his file and found he had a lengthy record of assaults. Had I been aware of this, I may have been less direct.

It was late as I traveled Highway 21 south, making up time. I did not want to be on back roads after dark. The road had five-foot ditches on either side. I rounded a curve and cattle covered the road—I braced for the crash.

Then the herd was behind me. My rearview mirror was full of cattle. Was it a dream, a wake-up call, or the luck of the Irish?

I did not mention the road full of cattle at morning coffee.

* * *

My arrival in Wenatchee was not the sole event at the time. The Goldmark libel trial had just opened in Okanogan court, with the national press observing. A local publisher had accused attorney John Goldmark and his wife, Sally, of being Communists. Goldmark sued for libel, and Judge Turner from Seattle heard the case.

Local citizens had strong political views, be they far right or far left. In the clerk's office I was once asked, "Are you Communist?"

My reply was, "No, I am a state employee."

Goldmark's libel trial lasted a month, so it was hard to find a room at the Caribou Inn. It was a minor hardship, but the Goldmark trial had no other impact on me. The Caribou Inn bar patrons had wild arguments over the trial. The jury found for Goldmark.

* * *

By November, golden colors spread to forests as the master painter worked. In short order Okanogan was a snowy wonderland and hazardous. With snow on the roads, I stayed overnight on trips north.

I had monthly report stops in Brewster, Omak, and on odd months in Oroville or Republic. I carried sixty cases up north. I combined the report days with field and collateral visits, which were visits to offenders' family, friends, or coworkers.

I had ten cases in Wenatchee—clients Dave had previously supervised. They were parole cases, having served prison time. Wenatchee was a small town, so Dave had known the families. With me they got a fresh start.

The Okanogan post had been vacant for a time, so I was in a roundup mode for months as I redeveloped supervision. My first letdown occurred just a week after my first report day.

A young man called Joe reported for supervision at Omak City Hall. He walked five miles to visit. I felt with him being so motivated that he would be successful. I even drove him home to show my concern.

The next Monday, I heard Joe had been arrested for stealing beer from a shed. Joe was motivated all right, but showed bad judgment, especially after being in court the prior week. Joe was sentenced to a ten-year term at the Washington State Reformatory in Monroe.

Joe used bad judgment, but I had not spoken with him about what would occur if he committed another crime. I vowed that in future meetings, I would tell people the consequences of committing new crimes.

* * *

In mid-November I met Sheriff Bob Nichols and Superior Court Judge Leahy. Dave and Sheriff Nichols had worked patrol together and were friends. I felt welcome, a part of law enforcement. Dave said that was only half correct, for in truth we also helped criminals.

Dave was the best interviewer I met in my career. In meetings, I was amazed at his ability to shift topics yet stay upbeat. Dave listened for a crisis, a pattern, denial, starry-eyed hope, or a surprise. Anything a client offered. He wanted his clients to think when they left.

His weakness was keeping records. Our office secretary said, "Keep your reports simple, as it will make them easier to type and read." I felt lucky to have started in a rural area, because, like my reports, life was simpler. I had time to grow and learn this new jigsaw puzzle. Yet keeping records was a burden, so I often heard, "Stay organized!"

Dave pointed out his files, which were a mess, and said, "You are to avoid this." I heard, "Do as I say, not as I do."

The law says if it was not written down it did not happen. A paper trail is needed to confirm reality, but that focus has unintended consequences. If records are the priority, staffers look backward rather than forward, and public safety suffers. I did my paperwork, but for me, process was not my purpose. Public safety was always my first priority.

Organization was emphasized differently in different places. For example, the Chelan County Courthouse was professional. Up north, in my territory, court was informal. I would sometimes arrive at Okanogan court to find that a sentencing had occurred before my report. I spent weeks clearing up unplanned court surprises.

* * *

The highways I drove had no passing zones and, as I drove, I was sometimes burdened by slow campers in front of me. I was not patient. To stay calm, I let my mind wander. I thought of good and bad schools. I thought of a pre-sentence report I had written for a client named Jim and the high school records I had reviewed for it.

Teachers had tested him for anti-social behavior in second grade. "Why test so young," I wondered, "and why this test?" No effort was ever made to correct the flaw. As the test results were restated year after year, they became a self-fulfilling prophecy.

I was lucky. Teachers had ignored my firebug tendencies. All my teachers knew we kids were wild and needed civilizing. Today, schools get passing grades even as children drop out.

Education is no longer a primary concern for parents. A gap exists between classroom and home. Latchkey kids are not born, but raised, the result of parents working to buy stuff, or to put food on the table. In either case, kids find homes vacant.

My mind continued to wander in the magical silence of the winter roads, and I wondered about the importance of addressing fear in society. I knew fear could motivate; it is a basic premise in criminal justice and is the rationale for public sentencing. Public sentencing was meant to deter miscreants and reaffirm the positive choices of others. But what is fear?

Fear is a learned emotion and also an instinctive reaction. With uncontrolled conditions, fear can ripen into terror until courage evaporates. The unknown is a driving force of fear in the human life cycle. As life paradigms shift, unknowns evolve, requiring new sets of life skills.

To do probation and parole work was to be an agent of change, and change brings anxiety into relationships. To reduce stress, I focused on a personal philosophy—success rests on choices. This was at times difficult, as the right path for clients seemed so clear to me. I learned to keep my mouth shut and allow others to make their own choices. Yet I knew that if my clients failed to make good choices, it would hurt public safety in the long term.

* * *

Public speaking is not my gift, so when Sheriff Wills asked me to talk at the Okanogan County Cattlemen's Association I had wanted to say no. But I had no excuse, so I agreed. I had nothing to say after a few months on the job.

Sheriff Wills was in a basement room at the Okanogan Café when I arrived. The room was full of talk as we moved up front. It died to silence as Wills introduced me.

"I am glad to be here," I lied.

My honesty improved as I said, "I'm here to listen," and sat down. I looked out at the quiet crowd, hoping a rancher would stand.

I was relieved when a rancher in the back told of his hardships. Others spoke of rustlers and hunters.

That afternoon, I had seen pre-sentence reports on a pair of Seattle hunters. Wills knew the court would not send hunters to prison. Therein was my lesson—never carry a hot potato if someone else is willing. The sheriff hit three birds with one stone: he educated me, he got a free lunch, and I was now out front instead of him. Wills had given me to his ranchers.

When the ranchers stopped talking, I thanked the room for listening. I heard later that I had given a great talk. I had spoken less than twenty words.

* * *

On the Saturday after my talk, I got a phone call. A parolee, Henry, was in the Okanogan County Jail. I rushed to review my file. It was full of violations and psychiatric reports. Henry had been diagnosed as a psychopath with a violent temper, and now he had been arrested for a burglary at a shop in Twisp. Henry had been found selling stolen tools off his truck in Omak.

In previous reviews, nothing in the file had jumped out. But that day it became clear Henry was a wild man. I asked Dave Schafer to join me for my first jail interview, but his schedule was full.

"You go interview Henry, then we can talk," he said. Dave's lack of interest worried me.

On Monday I headed north on Highway 97. I wanted a guide, a script. I was worried as I parked near the jail. I realized I did not have my format for violation reports; the outline was sitting on my desk in Wenatchee.

The jail lobby was empty except for a lone deputy working at a counter. Badge in hand, I stepped up. He was expecting me—he was the one who had called me on Saturday to tell me of the arrest.

We moved to a room with a plain wood table and two chairs, one wood, the other overstuffed. The floor was dirty. Green curtains hung on the high windows. A door to the alley was open and I felt a breeze. Sunlight streamed in.

Before I could close the alley door, a metal door on the back wall opened. I turned to face the prisoner. My mind went blank as to Henry's history.

A large man in a red-checked woolen shirt and jeans, hair covering his face, stood in the doorway. I thought, "What do I say?"

"This is Henry," the deputy said. He told Henry to sit, then closed the lobby door. We were alone.

Henry blinked in the bright light. He looked as if he had slept in a haystack. He stood in stocking feet and looked down on me, his shirt unbuttoned.

"Who are you?" Henry said, blinking as he sat in the wood chair.

"I've taken Wally's place," I replied.

A cool breeze reminded me the alley door was open. I looked away, trying not to give Henry any ideas. I moved to the stuffed chair. I dropped and I dropped. My arms were shoulder high after my free fall, my files all mixed up.

I was sweating. Things were not going well. I fumbled with my files as I looked up at Henry. He frowned.

"Relax," he said. "Are you new? Where's Wally?"

The Okanogan jail, which was crowded during picking season, was pressing in on Henry.

"Have you ever written a report?" he asked.

His head dropped as I said, "No."

He looked up.

"I'll write the report if you get me out of here quickly."

I nodded. "We have a deal."

Our deal was I would file the report quickly to get him out of his overcrowded cell, and he would dictate the report for me. Henry knew how the system worked; I didn't. I filled three pages as Henry talked. Henry quoted prison psych assessments from memory. I forgot all about the open door.

"You get copies of police reports," he said, and confirmed our deal. "You write the report quickly." I thanked him when we were finished.

With Henry in tow, I reported to the lobby desk. That upset the deputy. In the future, he said, I was to call him, because the rules said not to bring a prisoner out of the visiting room. He was abrupt. I did not mention the open alley door.

In Wenatchee, I wrote my report using the format I had left on my desk. I heard praise telling me I wrote a good report.

My experience with Henry taught me that psychiatric labels are misleading. Labels are a shortcut. They send a generic message that is not specific to the individual, and so are often misused or misinterpreted.

Citizens assume prison is the worst place to be, but that is not always true. At times, it is worse in Okanogan County Jail, in apple season, when the cells are stuffed.

* * *

I found my work was largely random. The word system was a misnomer. In theory, citizens are treated equally, but in reality no justice system in existence can function unerringly, as each entity consistently focuses on its own mission.

Police and other justice entities fill specific needs. Police do the arrests, courts enforce values to keep communities safe, and those of us working in corrections carry out court directives by way of prison custody or probation supervision. Each element depends on another's actions.

Elected officials are essential to the system, as they write laws, approve funds, and provide oversight. Funding represents priority, so an agency's effort corresponds to its funding levels. Most officials have a love-hate relationship with criminal justice and pay attention to it only to get and stay elected.

The system's public goal is to deter illegal acts and build public trust. But I found that victims were seldom made whole; a court conviction cannot reverse a victim's loss. A basic element missing from the formal justice process is the victim.

The justice system is debated in terms of good or bad, black or white, as citizens apply their moral attitudes on hurtful behavior to crime. The public still thinks punishment stops crime. "I hope you learn!" is the public cry. Yet we ignore that most crooks are never caught and therefore never punished.

* * *

In December 1963, Herb Roll and I drove to Seattle for new staff orientation. We agreed we would have great jobs if we could pass the mandatory six-month probation. After working for two months, we had seen few written guidelines. Instead, judgment and integrity were highlighted daily.

These simple attributes were characteristic of the rural life; city staffers carried a harder edge. The size of an office was basic to the disparity in the office environments. We heard of disputes in Seattle and Tacoma between offices and police, the courts, and the board. The conflicts within our agency were legendary.

While driving and discussing a weighty topic with Herb, I got lost. It was dark and raining heavily. Confused, I looked at street signs for help.

I found trouble on Marginal Way. I saw a car stop in front of us. I hit my brakes, our front end dropped, and I rear-ended the other car. The car I hit was undamaged and drove away toward the airport. My state car was totaled. I called the state patrol and admitted I was not paying attention.

I imagined my career was lost as I called Bob Lizee to report my accident. Yet no one was hurt, so he said it was no big deal. He told me to see Bill Young and get another car. Young gave Herb the keys.

I was not allowed to drive, but that was okay. I had had my fill of Seattle. I taught a traffic safety session during orientation.

Within a week, Herb's parked car was sideswiped at a meter. It was not Herb's fault, but Bill Young had a bias against Spokane drivers and saw the accident as Herb's fault. His accident took pressure off me; he joined me in the outcast class. Bill gave the next car to Judy Smith, who arrived at orientation as a new hire for Spokane. She covered eastern Washington's female cases. Bill told us, "Only Judy drives." Judy took Young's order seriously.

Orientation was on the fourteenth floor of the Smith Tower, with a view of Seattle and Elliott Bay.

Classes consisted of senior staff telling stories of their experiences. The basic message was that we were independent, but authority flowed down from courts or the board. We worked for public safety; when we helped offenders, that in turn protected public safety.

We heard about guidelines of conduct. Orientation reviewed agency procedures and policies, but it was clear there were few formalized written specifics.

On our last class day, we traveled to Olympia to visit the board. We met the members at the Institutions Building, which seemed small.

Seattle staff got rowdy with the board members. Tensions were heavy and childish. I saw wasted energy as staff argued, and I thought, "A house divided cannot stand." Our Olympia trip felt like a downer.

After orientation, Judy, Herb, and I headed home, up I-5 to I-90 east. It was late afternoon and soon dark. We cleared the pass and arrived in Ellensburg in fog. Judy disliked traffic and fog. It was thirty miles per hour into Spokane. Judy would not give up the wheel.

The rift between the board and field workers that I saw in Olympia surfaced again at a meeting in Moses Lake. Harris Hunter, the board chairman, was red-faced as a staffer questioned board politics. George Parks, a member of the board who was trying to get agency staff to work for Governor Rosellini's re-election, banged his fist on a table.

I was shocked by that outburst, but the meeting continued as if nothing had happened.

When I returned to Wenatchee I asked Dave about the event. He said Parks was reacting to upcoming elections. The board was a political animal, Dave said, so who became governor could impact employment. Existing members of the board could be out of work when their terms ended.

* * *

It was a warm spring in 1964. I was comfortable and my probation period had ended.

Usually a female staffer in Spokane managed the female cases in eastern Washington. But Judy Smith transferred to Seattle, so for a time five women reported to me.

One challenge was a woman who had neither reported nor paid her restitution. Her name was Ruth, and she lived on the Okanogan River across from Judge Murray. He saw Ruth come and go. He was upset when a storeowner asked him to find out if Ruth had paid restitution. Murray was up for re-election in the fall, and he had mentioned Ruth when we met.

Ruth was a priority but was never at home. After my third visit, I asked Murray for a bench warrant.

Murray said no. He would not send a neighbor to jail.

Ruth had five dogs: two labs, two collies, and a terrier. The dogs had a ritual. When I stopped, the dogs would yap. When I reached the porch, they would settle down. I would knock and there would be no answer. When I retreated, the dogs would circle. My briefcase was my protection.

Once, I was in the car after another visit, and the dogs went wild as usual. "Did a curtain move?" I thought. I could have sworn a curtain moved.

"Ruth was home," Murray later told me. "She left after you left."

I asked him again for a warrant. Again he refused.

My luck with those dogs ran out on my next visit. As I pounded on Ruth's door, I saw a flash. A terrier bit my pant leg. I yelled. The dogs went wild. I swung my briefcase. I was not going to make it to my car.

The door opened. A woman in her mid-twenties stood in a bathrobe. The dogs calmed down.

She told me that her husband was gone. I was a stranger to her, so she had hidden. I had not left my card.

Ruth and I had a brief visit. I told her that I would not visit again. If restitution was not paid, or if she was not at city hall on report days, she faced jail. I did not mention Judge Murray.

* * *

Back in Wenatchee, I watched Dave interview. Reeder was best at field visits. We traveled in alternate weeks, going from town to town, farm to farm, or to food sheds. We would end evenings doing night visits to back-road bars.

If a client was drinking, it was a violation. We worked until midnight if we made an arrest. We were not armed, but I did not worry for our safety. We had the court's authority, and that was enough for compliance.

Reeder, once a Mormon missionary, was not shy. He told me that conduct counts. He was sometimes at odds with headquarters on the issue of accountability, but the local courts supported him. They did not take kindly to Olympia giving orders to local staffers.

Normally, bureaucrats avoided conflict with the court. Still, we needed influence beyond a big stick, more than the idea that bad things happen if a client failed to comply.

* * *

I thought I had lived but I had yet to fall off the turnip wagon. I needed to set limits for my clients while still showing them respect, but it was not automatic. Respect required that I develop a relationship, but I was embarrassed at the scope of our powers.

After all, our supervisory relationship with our clients was not between equals. We had a power role as enforcers of the courts, and it was easy to slip into the use of power.

To hedge against that tendency, I decided my role was not to make clients' choices for them. Instead I asked clients to comply with court conditions and emphasized the risks of failure.

It was no more complicated than telling a client, "If you jump out a second-story window, bad things happen." It was not personal, just reality. I felt that staff members who took a power stance took a lazy way out.

Bob sometimes intervened in cases, though at times his temperament interfered. He was a doer, not a philosopher. He suffered sitting.

I tended to wait and let reality press a point, so I was not as involved as Reeder. Schafer was even more distant than I was; he did not give advice. Dave figured his job was to monitor and to raise his clients' awareness.

I found that by being positive I often attained goals via clients' self-motivation, self-interest, or even greed. Clients choosing the right path moved toward success. After nine months my thinking matured and I saw work differently, just as the sun in the east gives more light over time.

* * *

J. Murphy, a Spokane staffer, was old guard. He had been offered the position of parole board secretary. He visited our office in mid-1964 seeking Dave's input. Dave told Murphy the current board would vanish with a new governor and Murphy would be out of work; his job was an election issue.

Murphy asked Dave if he would feed him inside news about regional staff if he went to Olympia. Dave said no.

Later, Dave said that my presence had limited Murphy, since Murphy had already committed to the Olympia job. Murphy had big goals and was stressed from working for Lizee. He wanted to get ahead, but lacked a college degree.

In 1964, Governor Al Rosellini also visited Wenatchee. Dave brought him to our office, his arm over Al's shoulder. Rosellini was heavily tanned and taller than I expected. Sparks flew in his presence. Dave was going to introduce Rosellini at a chamber of commerce luncheon.

Dave was quiet when he returned in mid-afternoon.

The next day, over coffee, Dave said Rosellini would lose the election. His veto of a parole board bill would cost him. Voters disliked the politically active board; the public associated the current board with all the crooks released from prisons.

Governor Rosellini and candidate Dan Evans both played the crime card to raise fears, then spoke of cutting crime to gain votes. Evans proposed funding more police; Rosellini proposed expanding education. Evans spoke of justice in terms of good and evil, and his view got the public's attention. Rosellini had the burden of office and growing crime rates. As Dave predicted, Dan Evans bested Rosellini that November. Evans won again in 1968 and 1972.

What would and would not work in corrections was a constant question I looked at with unease. Luckily, I had miles of roads in Okanogan County, so I had time to think.

* * *

The most human ability is to make choices. A professor at Gonzaga once said, "Man always selects the perceived good." If that is true, then perception is the main driver for behavior. But how could I change a client's perceptions?

Criminals act impulsively in the moment; mature logic is not an influence, and my caseload was mostly young men. Immaturity was to be expected.

"What is maturity?" I wondered, and how would I know it when I saw it? Maturity is a person's ability to function at his age level. There are types of maturity—social, physical, and emotional—so judging it gets quite complicated.

Old folks broke laws, but committed quiet crimes. The majority of my cases were young adults, middle-aged drunks, or burnt-out old-timers seeking to vanish and retire. Crime was often the result of bad influences.

Their usual refrain was simply, "Tell me what I have to do."

History is history. We cannot alter it, but we can learn from life's harsh lessons. Yet we have a capacity to block experiences if they are too painful, and the potential lesson can vanish.

In interviews, I tried to raise awareness. I stressed options and the importance of making good choices. I tried to sort out each client's way of thinking. I did not impose my views; we each must make our own choices, and people who are dependent on others lose that ability.

I used a client's vocabulary to increase my effectiveness. Vocabulary conveys one's level of perception and indicates our values and ability to change.

Clients with average intelligence saw my plan and flooded me with small, useless facts that didn't really explain anything about them or what they were really doing. I had to step back and select topics I felt were important for public safety: income, friends, plans, beliefs, or their methods of dealing with trouble.

I was annoying to clients, but I had no set program. When I supervised someone, he saw that punishment was alive and well in Washington. I worked to know where clients stood on primary topics.

If clients struggled with behavior, I forced them to focus by limiting their goals. This created small successes, and success bred success. Small victories assured future effort, as they created a good attitude that influenced decisions.

* * *

Brewster was on the Columbia River an hour north of Wenatchee. From Brewster, I could go north up the Okanogan valley. The Brewster chief of police, Bea, taught me a lesson.

Chief Bea was friendly and helpful. Middle-aged and six feet tall, he was sharp. He was a great source of information but he both gave and got. His queries were often to assess if I knew what was going on. It seemed he knew facts that I did not.

One cold morning brought new snow. The roads north were slick, so I was in a hurry when I met with Bea. He asked me about a man named Keith, who I had met the week before at city hall. I offered to buy Bea coffee, but wanted to get on the road.

"How is Keith doing?" Bea asked again.

Keith was a bit slow, but I had thought he would stay out of trouble. He had a wife and a baby.

Bea did not drop the topic, so I figured I had better listen. Bea used Keith as a lesson that day as he talked about people assuming things.

"What is his point?" I wondered.

I gave in and decided to visit Keith on my way out of town.

He lived two blocks up on Main Street. It was cold, and the snow was a foot high on the path to his cinder block house next to a machine shop. I knocked lightly and no one answered. I hit the door harder.

The door cracked open and Keith peered out, wrapped in a blanket. On his head was a blue knit sea cap. The room was dark. My eyes adjusted and I saw he was fully clothed. I saw shadows and smelled sour milk. Keith's wife and baby were in the bed under blankets. With no sunlight, the house was bitter cold; they had only body heat. A cupboard on the wall was empty. Keith had not mentioned that he had no money when we visited at city hall. He likely felt he had trouble already.

They were freezing. I told Keith I would get help, and I found Bea, who located emergency food and wood. My slippery trip north was now unimportant. Instead, my first stop was public assistance, where I collected an emergency draft for the family so they could buy food and pay for heat.

Many of us benefit from families, good schools, and good-paying jobs. Yet such is not reality for everyone. Keith's church had defellowshipped him, and his own family could not help for fear of their own banishment. He had no social network.

Citizens use biblical values to judge criminal acts and, since sin is universal, everyone considers themselves experts. But being morally rotten does not mean someone is a criminal, and vice versa. For instance, greedy folk seldom cross the line, or they have lawyers who find loopholes in laws or change laws to meet their needs.

I learned early that good supervision required teamwork within the community. Keith's isolation was a crisis until his town was made aware and stepped in to help. Bea found work for Keith at the metal shop, which assisted in creating a help system.

Living miles from cases, I was compelled to use others' eyes and ears. Family members, employers, a good friend, or the police acted as collateral helpers in my supervision.

In rural communities, life was less complicated, so behavior was easier to identify. Crime disrupts the status quo. Citizens cared little about abstract crime, but crime was personal from a victim's point of view. With the likely exceptions of murder, sex crimes, and drug or alcohol abuse, the truth is that most crimes go unsolved. Prisons fill up with easy-to-catch offenders with dependencies.

People want justice to set wrongs right, but life is not always fair. On one side of town police made arrests, while on another they were assisting citizens. Most rural police were salt of the earth, but a few were not if no one was watching.

Policemen knew who was in town, and friends naturally wanted friends to do well and succeed. This mutually beneficial situation allowed clients time to reform. Yet I saw conflict in our imperfect world.

Buck was a town marshal, and he worked alone. He was heavyset, middle-aged, and a southern type who chewed tobacco. He did not change his mind or his shirt.

He wore wide red suspenders and carried a cattle prod as his nightstick. He was always ready to use it on drunks, or those who might "resist" arrest. Buck was a redneck. I got angry listening to him. How fair was a justice system if Buck was included? Still, he was my eyes and ears, so I met him and I bought lunch and coffee.

Buck talked and I listened on my trips to town. I gave him my Wenatchee phone number.

"You call me collect, any time, with questions," I told him.

Buck never called. I told my cases, "He knows about you."

I awaited a report that Buck had harassed a client, but no report ever came. Yet his presence in the system meant our world was imperfect. That said, Buck dealt with loggers or orchard workers raising hell in town every day, with no backup.

One man I admired was Omak Police Chief Cleghorn. Cleghorn was tough as a bent nail and looked good in a uniform. Curly white hair framed his leathery face and steel gray eyes. He was a talker who had worked as a logger and mill worker, and he had been chief of police for fifteen years.

Locals liked his quick wit and ready smile. I liked to ride with him when I stayed in town overnight because, unlike Buck, he was social. I joined him from just after six o'clock until the taverns emptied in east Omak. It was a chance for me to discover Omak and get a feel for the town's tempo.

I learned that police work was mostly boring but for minutes very stressful. The trick was not to overreact; slow and steady was the best prevention.

Chief Cleghorn walked through taverns before closing time, showing patrons he was on the lookout. Likely DWI candidates would find him at their car.

"Can I call a cab?" he would ask them. "No arrest tonight, your kids need your money."

If you were new in town, Cleghorn directed you to employment or had free advice on where to avoid trouble. If you were trouble, he told you of a town down the road more to your liking. When citizens saw Cleghorn, they felt safe. Night rides with him kept me out of trouble.

* * *

I held a report day at the Omak police station. I saw thirty clients, one of whom was a Colville Indian named Dick. Dick was twenty-eight but looked fifty. It was good that he reported; what was bad was that he was drunk! I arrested him and since he was a happy drunk he went quietly. The next day when we talked he was sober and shaky.

He told me that I would not have known of his drinking had he not reported.

I said, "The next time you report drunk, you go to jail, and I give a report to the judge to revoke your probation." Dick was an unhappy fellow.

The next report day he was drunk again. I arrested him and wrote a report to Judge Murray. I wrote that Dick was without question an alcoholic.

I quoted Dick, writing, "His drinking is the problem."

He would not stop drinking, so he would have to go to prison. Dick asked Murray to remove the alcohol restrictions from his probation.

I mentioned that he was thinking about the rules. If the drinking restriction was removed he would likely be successful. Murray agreed and dropped drinking as a condition as long as Dick stayed crime free.

Months passed and Dick's probation ended. I visited his ranch with discharge papers in hand. His mother told me Dick was found dead in a ditch the week before.

I knew that he would still be alive if he had been in prison. I was of no help to Dick by giving him the green light to drink. Never again did I accept a drunken Indian stereotype.

* * *

Okanogan's economy was orchards, logging, and ranching, so it was impacted by seasonal cycles. On back roads, the big world vanished and I was in God's country. Staff meetings brought me back to the real world.

A big event in Okanogan County was Omak Stampede Days. It was a crazy time; visitors arrived for a rodeo, Indian stick games, and a suicide race. Stampede Days brought visitors from all over, even Canada. Powwow encampments of Indian tribes ensured the Stampede's success. There were drums and dancing into the night, and streets filled with Stampede spirit.

Spring arrived in the Okanogan as major issues over sovereignty flared up on the Colville Reservation between the Colville tribe and Washington State. The Bureau of Indian Affairs gave me federal marshal power to arrest. I had limited tribal members on state supervision; federal judges handled most reservation crimes.

Francis was an Indian who drank too much. One night he took the Omak city water truck to visit a girl. The large truck was visible everywhere in Omak, so Francis was quickly arrested and taken to court.

After court, Sheriff Wills ignored Francis's probation status. One deputy drove Francis on a sundown parole into Canada—a sentence was given to satisfy the law, but Francis was shipped out and told not to come back or he would be arrested on sight. Wills screwed up my paperwork. I had papers, but no Francis. Both the sheriff and the judge wanted Francis to be somebody else's problem.

Francis corrected the error by beating deputies back to Omak and again took the water truck. I saw Francis afterward in Omak's jail, and submitted my paperwork.

Francis was a happy-go-lucky man and was made a trustee on Omak's garbage truck. He worked hard, so upon release from jail he was hired by the City of Omak. Within days, he took the water truck again.

Francis was arrested and thrown in Chelan County Jail to wait for transport to prison. Judge Murray had not needed my report.

I went to talk to Francis, but the visiting room was full so I visited Francis in his cellblock. We talked through the jail staff shift change before I yelled, "Key up!"

Jail staffers had not been told I was in a cellblock.

I yelled again, "Key up!" Nothing.

Francis sat laughing. He laughed, bent over, until I finally got out.

Months later, Francis called from Wenatchee's bus station. I visited him at the station. He was thinner, but smiling. We agreed to meet in Omak. He would stay with an aunt. On my next trip north I learned Francis had again stolen the water truck.

Wills drove Francis to a border crossing, to a Royal Canadian Mounted Police captain who owed him a favor. The captain took Francis far into northern Canadian Indian country. Francis remained on my caseload, but I did not see him again.

* * *

After the 1964 election, Dan Evans appointed a blue-ribbon group to study state agencies. The studies lasted three years, far below my radar. His effort was approved of in Olympia, as it also reviewed the parole board.

The last parole board reform before Evans had occurred in the 1930s, a time of strong local government, when power stayed at local courthouses. In 1946, Governor Langlie had centralized political power in agencies in Olympia. Rosellini had continued Langlie's efforts over his three terms.

In my orientation class, harsh statements had been directed to board members. I had been glad to leave for Wenatchee. Friction grew among the ranks of state agencies. In the east we sought public safety; a central boss was not very important. It seemed that political forces existed to bring us grief.

In 1964 I transported a case to King County, so I had the chance to tour both the jail and the Seattle office. Supervisor Bill Young must have forgotten about my driving, because he asked me to transfer into Seattle. I said no.

In Seattle, I saw unhappy staff members memorizing face books—folders of loose-leaf summary pages of cases. They would be tested on their memorization of the face books. I only used the books to find addresses on field visits; I had never been tested. In Seattle, testing allowed researchers at the University of Washington to rate staffers based on their level of case knowledge.

Testing produced hard data to rate staffers on supervision. Knowing a face book showed you knew your cases; not knowing the book meant you did not. The results were included in yearly reviews, so testing was a big deal.

Yet studying face books allowed no time to monitor clients, see their employers, or visit police. The staff focused on history, not on offenders' current or future behavior.

* * *

In Wenatchee, to make a mistake was to learn. To repeat it raised eyebrows. It was not work for free spirits, as consistency was essential. We spoke the truth and kept our word. Humor helped with the seriousness. If the humor was self-directed it helped keep us sane.

Dave had gone to the same high school as a man named Brown. Brown was fifty-four years old and angry. He went to prison for a burglary. His crime: he had broken into a shed and taken back tools that a neighbor had borrowed and not returned.

Brown admitted to the break-in in a report made to the sheriff. Deputies feared trouble so they arrested Brown. Brown argued with the prosecutor who reviewed his case, so he was charged. The neighbor would not drop the charges.

A jury found Brown guilty based on his statements and the court ordered him to stay off the neighbor's land. Brown argued and his probation vanished.

Being a bonehead, he went to prison, so a parole board set his actual prison term. He refused to see the board, so they set his term at the maximum ten years and planned to review his case in a year.

The next year Brown would not budge and was sent to isolation until he agreed to meet with the board. Isolation meant months in a blackout cell. Brown refused to say uncle and see the board, earning him the title Siberian Brown.

In the third year the board met with Brown in his cell. They granted his release, but he was angry. Since Dave knew him, which was a conflict of interest, I was assigned to supervise him.

Brown lived in a boarding house for a time. To protest, he sat with his back to me as he reported.

"Parole rules do not say how you have to sit," I said. "As long as you report, I will see your backside."

I could not see if he frowned or smiled.

Because of his attitude I told Brown that he would not last the week.

He replied, "You're nuts, and I will prove you wrong."

He won that one. The months passed. I reported, I asked questions, and he replied yes or no.

Brown enjoyed saying, "I am still out and you're all wet."

Dave seemed pleased about it. Reeder sat backward on visits to my office and laughed.

In May, Brown found a Rolex watch on the street and turned it in to me. An attorney down the hall had a client who had lost the $400 watch. It impressed the attorney that an ex-con had returned it, and he told a local newspaper.

The Wenatchee paper ran a story on Brown's honesty. Brown arrived at his next report with the paper in his hand and turned his chair. He had made his point. I no longer heard harsh words, and I allowed him to move to his farm.

Brown worked his farm and walked twenty miles to report. He said he was not a crook. In 1967, on a haystack, he had a heart attack. I wished Saint Peter luck in dealing with Brown. I hoped Peter had a sense of humor.

* * *

We represented our agency to citizens who knew little about the courts and our agency's rules. When we dealt with citizens it was most often in a crisis event, so the public feared criminals and our system. They often reacted with submission or by pushing back; if I saw anger, I did not push back. Their anger was useful because angry people spoke truth. I praised honesty because it took courage. Courage was facing one's fears and the unknowns that caused them. Above all I wanted to keep communications open.

We ensured compliance with probation conditions and oversaw restitution. Olympia was the center of our universe, with the authority to tax and the power to shift and allocate funds.

Sentencing laws in 1964 allowed for regional diversity between rural and urban areas. The drums of fairness sounded in 1966—some citizens sought statewide fairness because more urban blacks were in prison under indeterminate sentencing.

Reformers compared the black prison population to the number of blacks in the general population and saw the variance. Urban officials sought reform through Evans's blue-ribbon committee.

Sentencing reform was a hot topic. Soon, the tail wagged the dog. Evans wanted the efficiency of a one-stop agency and control of the Great Society programs. Sentencing reforms had to wait as Department of Social and Health Services legislation moved forward.

Criminals could not vote, but crime shaped voters' opinions. The public figured, "Why help crooks if law-abiding citizens had needs?" Evans helped the sick, the elderly, and the poor. Society punished sinners who committed crimes.

Citizens lacking knowledge had mixed feelings about field staffers' role. We had ties to police, yet helped crooks—it made no sense to most people. Their "Oh God!" response, in time, grew legs and a voice.

* * *

Fred Finsley arrived in Olympia as director of probation and parole—better known as field chief—in 1964. He was smooth, well dressed, and impressive, a been-there-done-that sort. He was an agent of change with a message: Get on board or leave. Fred, a lawyer and past chairman of California's parole board, spoke with resolve. Rumors flew from day one after he announced reporting format changes at a regional staff meeting.

Once, baffled at a staff meeting as senior staff members appeared confused, I asked a dumb question about why they wanted to confuse staff.

Fred replied, "John, why ask dumb questions?" He said he, not staff, set agency agendas. He was the boss.

I shut up. I disliked him for a week, maybe two. But with Fred, it was not personal. His goal was efficiency. He was on a mission to push us beyond social work. He put an end to flowery reports and changed how we viewed clients. When we reported performance or charged violations we had to give evidence. No hunches or gut feelings were allowed. He did not buy social work theories or mysteries understood only by the few staffers with master's degrees.

Fred ended jail therapy arrests, when clients were arrested as a warning to change behavior. He said to be less involved; helping was not our priority. There would be no social work or police work going forward—we were to think and act as a legal entity. He aligned field service with superior courts to ensure strong local support for us after he left.

Fred knew he had a brief window to make change. He used his time to gain line staff support. We newer staffers adjusted. We had no history, no dog in the fight, nothing to unlearn, no sense of loss. Senior staffers struggled, yet there was no turning back.

Fred reinvented our culture with this abrupt change, so for some time things were difficult. Fred was a top-down boss, which made the transition even harder as he channeled power from Olympia to the regions.

Fewer staffers invested in our historic mission of public safety. Fred could have walked softly but that was not his style. He knew what he wanted.

Fred ended the parole board's already-dying spoils system in which elected officials hired the people who helped them get elected. He found loyal supporters in regional staff as he stopped the practice of Olympia reviewing field reports. After regional review, reports went to the courts or the board, so power shifted to regions because they had the final review. In eastern Washington, Lizee and Prideaux supported Fred; he had a direction.

West-side staffers resisted. The University of Washington lost its research network as the new report system replaced the traditional narrative of a case's family, education, and employment with a report on the crime or incident. The UW could now only collect that kind of information at prison intake instead of through monitoring staff reports.

With changes ongoing, a Spokane staffer transferred out and a job opened in Spokane. In 1964, I transferred to Spokane and rejoined friends and regained my social life.

It was hard to leave Wenatchee. I was part of my cases' lives; their success was my success. I felt sorry for the clients I left because my insight was no longer available to them. A Caesar complex was easy to grow.

I thanked Schafer for being open to my peering eyes. He had earned my respect. He had known within a week that my stay would be brief in Wenatchee. He helped me even though he did not care a twit for life beyond Wenatchee. His questions had kept me thinking, and Reeder had shown energy and personal commitment.

* * *

Since 1889, Washington State's population had grown, driven by lumber, Alaskan gold, shipbuilding, Boeing, and technology. After 1952 most state agencies hired via civil service, so veterans got hiring preference. Once the post-1952 hires were promoted to key managerial and leadership roles, we were led by GI Bill college types.

These college types reacted to cronyism and political hires. The parole board, as a tiny agency, was not required to follow civil service hiring guidelines. Five board members and a chairman served five-year terms once selected by the governor and confirmed by the Senate.

The board's function was to set minimum terms, establish parole rules, and direct field staff. Members worked in teams of two at prisons. Based on board rules, they could adjust inmates' parole eligibility or revoke parole status.

The board modified policies and operations and hired staff to supervise probation cases and to insure compliance with conditions set by the superior court. The board also hired the chief probation and parole officer to direct field staff.

The chief interacted with board members to ensure that staffers focused on public safety. The rub was that staffers resented politics and sought buffers to ensure professionalism from a board that was a political entity.

In 1962 a bill was passed, not supported by Governor Rosellini, to remove field staff from the board in that legislative session. Field staffers' move to the Department of Institutions had been supported by the UW School of Social Work. Transfer of field headquarters to Olympia in 1954 had caused the board to become more involved in field business.

Existing board members did not see themselves as a problem and resented the suggestion, as did Governor Rosellini. Tensions remained even after Dan Evans became governor. He named new board members when previous members' terms expired.

Finsley was our boss during this transition period from 1965 into 1966, as the pot boiled on with agency changes and sentencing reform. There was talk about the fairness of rehabilitation theory.

The medical model theory was a cornerstone in the prisons at the time; the premise was that offenders were essentially sick and needed treatment, and we were the help agent. Parole and probation work stayed hidden as the silent service.

Fred's error was that he saw probation as rehabilitation, not punishment. Fred lacked a killer instinct. We entered an era of punishment as crime rates grew along with the economy. A crime committed by his son was used to force Fred out; they said if he could not raise a child properly then he couldn't be trusted to run a department. But his shadow lingered.

Spokane
1964–1966

I returned to Spokane in December 1964. Bob Lizee was the region supervisor for Walla Walla, Pasco, Yakima, Wenatchee, and Spokane—a territory that ranged from the Cascade Mountains to Idaho, and from Oregon to the Canadian border.

Bob was forceful, quick tempered, and liked king's English. He expected his staff to protect public safety and work with the courts, prosecutors, and police. His staffers were white, mostly males, with a degree of urban smugness.

John Prideaux ran the Spokane office by Lizee's book. He asked me to work Spokane and Pend Oreille counties. I was up north one day each week. I liked the assignment since it gave me a break from my hectic routine. Spokane's pace was rapid, and I had to focus to avoid embarrassing goofs. I valued my road time—it reduced office stress as I drove alone with my thoughts.

The office was in a French-style courthouse on Broadway. Four days a week I worked in the courthouse offices above the county sheriff's office. Prosecutors were on the floor below. We were at the center of the justice system.

Our office was on the fourth floor. On the left coming out of the elevator was Judge Kelly's court. On the right was our door. Most courtrooms were in the courthouse, but Judge Kelly seemed to like being off the beaten path, though traffic in the foyer was still heavy on court days.

I settled in quickly. Our office was one open room; eight-foot panels of milky glass and wood standing four feet short of the ceiling created cubicles. On the left were windows, on the right a law library wall. A bench up front served as a waiting area by the receptionist's desk. Overflow visitors sat on a bench in the hallway.

Seniority determined the office assignments, so senior staffers had windows. My cubicle was up front with the library wall at my back.

Staff meetings and our large caseloads drove the pace of the office. Chatter mixed with the blue haze of cigarette smoke above the partitions. I overheard conversation and other muffled noises.

Our office mood varied depending on who stayed in the office and who traveled out to Whitman, Adams, Pend Oreille, Stevens, or Lincoln counties. We attended court days, pleadings, and sentencings.

Three of the twelve staffers in our office were secretaries. We each had different personalities, politics, and social views. We were unified in one aspect—our mission was to protect the public. In Seattle, staffers' opinions on public safety differed. Seattle police were less helpful and Seattle newspapers chased headlines. Spokane was a different world.

* * *

My first pre-sentence in Spokane was Richard, a seventy-year-old retired federal employee. He had pled to fraud for false statements on loan forms. The first loan had started his spice and seasoning distribution business.

He and his attorney visited before I had reviewed his files. My cubicle was a tight fit for the big men. In his dark suit and tie, with white hair, I at first thought Richard was the attorney. Yet looking in his eyes I saw a broken man. He was worried about his ill wife. Her health had prompted his plea, but Richard's attorney wanted to try the case. I said his attorney could only submit his written input to the judge, and both men left let down.

I headed downstairs to find Deputy Prosecutor Dick Wrenn. He was in his office with a dolly stacked with boxes.

"Are you good at math?" he asked.

"Not very," I replied.

He pushed the dolly down the hall and into an office with a long table.

"I'm sorry I did not see the plea coming," he said. "I cannot release files but you can work with them here. You look this over, and then we can talk."

In the boxes were contracts and billings. I reviewed files to get the scope of the crime and restitution. The material was in chronological order, but that was the extent of Dick's progress. I had to review all the documents and figure out the restitution that was owed, including compounded interest.

Richard and the firm had a four-year history. The first loan had paid for trips to trade shows and for direct marketing. The loan was $20,000, but was factored. He never sold enough products to pay the interest, and his debt grew. With interest upon interest, Richard's obligation grew to $250,000.

The manager and regional vice president of the loan firm prosecuting Richard visited to discuss restitution. They painted their picture and talked fast. I asked them to submit their input in writing.

Richard's assets were his business, a savings account, a car, and his home. Federal bankruptcy law protected homes but not as part of restitution. I saw Richard as the victim in the case and believed a court trial would reveal that fact. I sent a report to Wrenn with a paper trail to support my conclusion.

Wrenn met with the managers and the firm took Wrenn's offer. Richard got probation and paid a $500 fine with $1 of restitution.

* * *

Judges in Spokane were accessible and Senior Judge Ralph Foley especially. Foley was a tall, white-haired icon. He had the look of a judge. He had been a legislator in the 1930s and had written parts of the Board of Prison Terms and Paroles Act. His son Tom was a congressman representing eastern Washington.

Judge Foley worked at his own pace on paperwork and would stop court proceedings if any probation staff needed his time. In chambers, Foley would stretch and ask me about my family before getting down to business. If court was not in session, visits might last an hour.

I interrupted his court once, and the bailiff, Gil, called me forward. Judge Foley adjourned the court and I walked past angry eyes into chambers; attorneys dislike breaks. Foley paced, stretched, and talked. He complained about a lawyer who could not find his point, and how his bench was hard on old bones.

After ten minutes of Foley stretching, I walked out and saw frowns. An attorney putting out a cigarette in the hall smiled; some attorneys do like breaks.

Foley was a history buff and had stories of the early days. Once, he spoke of train travel and how Spokane lost its influence.

Prior to the 1940s, legislators took trains to legislative sessions.

Trains left Spokane for Olympia days before the sessions. Lobbyists also rode the trains, so deals often occurred before the trains topped the Cascade Mountains, well before Seattle members boarded. The trains were a moving caucus.

Spokane benefited from the train arrangement as cross-party loyalties developed, but road and air travel changed that life. Caucus trains became history. Wide-open Spokane lost its importance and influence in Olympia.

At the time, Spokane was populated by out-of-work miners, loggers, and farm workers, who did not vote. Political power shifted to cities with jobs, trade, and stable workforces, like Seattle and Tacoma. Eastern legislators held some sway for a while because of their seniority on committees.

In the 1960s, Spokane's court was an island of calm. Local judges were peaceful in the face of a broader political storm. Willard J. Roe, William H. Williams, Hugh Evans, Jack J. Lally, Ralph Edgerton, and Raymond Kelly all talked to our staff.

Each judge had a personality, and their black robes had an aura that demanded attention. An agency directive said to limit our input, but judges sought input even if they ignored it.

* * *

Wenatchee seemed like a dream, but it also felt like only yesterday that I had walked into that first office. John F. Kennedy had already been dead for a year in 1964.

At home on Ermina Street, life was good. I was welcome. Most of my siblings were out of the house. Mary was married, Dave was in Seattle, and Jim was in Spokane. Denny was overseas in Korea. Patty was at home with Mom and Dad when I returned.

I had a job and friends, so my life was mellow. Dad was now manager at McPherson Heating Supply. His long hours in the cold and the heavy lifting were gone now that Dad was the boss. He liked his job; he was relaxed.

My mother was still in housewares at Valu-Mart. She didn't need to work, but enjoyed her friends and the contact with customers and buying things for her grandkids. Jim worked in Valu-Mart's warehouse.

I lived at home and paid room and board, which helped my folks. Summer weekends included visits to our cabin at Hayden Lake. Dad and Mom took trips to Reno three times a year.

Mom and Patty played bingo twice a week at Knights of Columbus. Patty also bowled and led her league with an average of two hundred. However, what Patty really wanted was a job.

My own social life was bar-hopping with friends on Friday nights. When I was out on the town I shifted talk away from crime and punishment. I had a social life that was not tied to work. Friends knew my job title, but few really knew what I did. They sometimes read about cases in the newspaper and asked about them. Typically we did not talk about failures. Once a client was sentenced, the book was shut and that matter was closed.

My job put money in my pocket, so I did not count pennies. I turned twenty-seven years old in March 1965; I felt that the clock was ticking, so I started trying to fit in romance.

I was always looking for the right person. I liked to compare, so I felt that if dating one woman was good, dating seven was better. I kept up that pace for months, and the number of my dates grew. I enjoyed life in 1965.

One night at a Catholic Youth Organization barn dance on Mount Spokane I met Kathleen Santorsola. By our second date, I knew she was right. I lost interest in others. I wanted to get serious, but Kathy, with better judgment, was skeptical. We dated for a year before Kathy said, "Yes."

* * *

In the courthouse I made ties with prosecutors, which made work easier. I picked up eighty-five cases in order to equalize the workload among staff. Most staffers transferred cases carefully, but a few dumped them on me without any explanation, so the new caseload was a challenge.

There was also officer of the day (OD) duty that rotated among the staff. The OD was responsible for covering office emergencies.

In Spokane, my co-workers were Herb Roll, Wally Karnitz, Bob Banta, Jim Northrop, and Linda Chapman. Each was helpful in showing me local social service resources, and I knew help was just a phone call away.

Herb Roll was friendly, single, and reserved. He assembled electronics kits and had a home library. He was promoted and transferred to Olympia in 1965, shortly after I arrived. Herb moved to a supervisor job in Seattle in 1968, then quit the next year to attend Washington State University for a master's degree and PhD in social work. He later taught at Eastern Washington University.

Roll was replaced in Spokane by Jerry Savland. Jerry was a retired colonel who had served in Patton's Seventh Army. He was fifty-something, set in his ways, and hard of hearing. He carried himself with a sense of command but was not a patient man. He usually called me kid or boy.

Wally Karnitz was a part-time minister, a family man, and a social worker. He struggled with our job's dual responsibilities to police and assist our cases. Wally had been my predecessor in Wenatchee, so we had lots to talk about and he loved to talk. I limited my contact with Wally because his lengthy conversations put me behind on paperwork. But he did know the local resources.

Bob Banta was the joker. An English major, he grasped the work easily but liked practical jokes. An ongoing war of jokes existed between Bob and Prosecutor George Kain. Bob and Kain could have filled a book with their banter but I was wary. Bob worked well with police and offenders.

Banta carried both a valley and a city caseload. He was from Millwood, so he lobbied for an office in the valley, which he eventually got. Bob also worked Whitman County during the 1966 WSU unrest.

Linda Chapman, a Whitman College graduate, hired on during my time in Wenatchee. I first met her in Wenatchee and had dinner with her and her parents in Pateros. Chapman took Judy Smith's place when Judy moved to Seattle in 1964. Linda and I had a special bond because we shared a similar learning curve and a birthday.

Working in a male-dominated agency, Linda found herself an inside-outsider. She worked hard to be professional; she was businesslike and always well dressed.

Jim Northrup and I rode to work together as we both lived in north Spokane. He had been born in Colville, Washington, and lobbied for a Colville office. Jim was the office cop, hard-nosed and long in the tooth. He was old school; changes caused him heartburn. Jim had his issues and was not a patient man, but he was adamant about public safety.

Jim was a captain in the National Guard and on active duty most summers. He took a hunting vacation each fall. He had been a medic on Spokane's police ambulance unit, so he used medical terms in reports, which drove secretaries crazy.

* * *

In Spokane, resource agency visits and police contacts were in offices, not in cafés as they had been in Wenatchee. So I did not take café breaks, opting for the coffee brewed in a back office. There was a rolling coffee break whenever staff members had time.

Over coffee, we discussed cases, court, police, resources, or sporting events. When there wasn't time, the cup moved on. The open break system had its troubles—if we were not careful, coffee breaks consumed an entire day and nothing got done. Wally especially liked his cup of joe and the talking that went with it. I was abrupt when Wally visited.

Coffee breaks were also on-the-job training sessions, a time to ask or answer questions. We used these dialogues to come to consensus on issues. I focused on casework and had no interest in gossip, yet the rumors helped unite staff and we grew to share values.

Leadership in Olympia had changed when the board pushed Bob Austin out in 1962. Fred Finsley, who had hired on from California while I was in Wenatchee, spurred a lot of rumors with his changes, so we had plenty to talk about on our coffee breaks in Spokane.

Fred noticed the disparity between views from the east and west, law and order vs. social work, central vs. regional oversight, and professional staff vs. political appointees.

Fred resisted Olympia managers with master's degrees and that view was a hard pill for social workers and Olympia to swallow. The board did not want the issue of professionalism raised in the legislature. Seattle had been home to the central office until it moved to Olympia, and both the University of Washington and Seattle University had sought professionals in the field staff in the interest of justice and fairness.

Historically, the schools had influenced our report formats, but Finsley wanted reports to be a decision vehicle for courts, not a research tool. Reports had a precision and structure. If reports were below standard, they were rejected in Olympia and not sent to judges. Rewriting reports upset the courts.

Fred questioned the medical model's validity; he pushed for civil rights and rehabilitation. He used legal terms such as "conditions" and "precedent." The superior courts liked Fred and his legalese. Finsley said the public needed to know what we did to ensure their safety.

Offenders and staff would both be accountable in this new paradigm. Fred battled the Olympia grammar patrol that believed report review was more important than face-to-face field supervision. He eliminated the requirement calling for a headquarters signature on reports. Some folks believed headquarters' reason for existing vanished the day Fred made that decision.

Fred told Olympia staffers to reinvent their mission. He wanted policies that would standardize best practices in fieldwork. He said, "Fixing nouns and verbs does not create policy."

Fred also got us a pay raise. While I felt that staff benefited from his vision, I disagreed with him on other changes such as report formats and oversight changes. The Olympia staff did not forget his treatment of them. If it had been up to them, Fred would have been gone.

Bob Lizee and John Prideaux liked Fred, as he increased the regional power of Spokane, Tacoma, and Seattle, and made the reporting system faster and more focused. Then rumors spread that Fred would limit our power to arrest. Fred felt staff abused that power, which was a slap in our face.

This rumor hit the Spokane staff hard, as many felt the ability to arrest was essential to public safety. We worked in a rule-based scheme, and we made a promise to our clients: Do right or lose your freedom. Some staffers were ready to revolt over the power of arrest issue, while social workers saw it as a victory.

The reality was that staffers planned arrests, talked to police, and asked for backup. Supervisors played a part in our arrest plans, so their approval was merely symbolic.

Before I arrested a client I had to be convinced they had violated rules of probation or were a public risk. I could hold a case in jail for nine days without a report. On the tenth day, I had to file an arrest report with the board or the court.

If I released the client before day ten, I would report my arrest in the next progress report cycle. We called this a therapeutic arrest, and staffers used it for minor violations to gain a client's attention. It was a lazy way out for staffers, and yearly audits exposed such actions.

However, Fred said audits were not sufficient. He wanted warrants to be issued by a supervisor. Without that limit, Fred said, staffers had too much power. He said staffers should explain their reasons in a review before an arrest was made.

* * *

Coffee breaks got longer as Fred's changes came to pass. He limited staff's ability to do high-risk activities like arrests. He instituted a rehabilitation system, and the conditions of supervision narrowed and got more specific. Fred limited staff options and centralized decision-making to promote consistency. There was less direct court involvement as bureaucratic processes filled the court's role. Some agency policy was written to limit headlines. Social workers liked Fred, but law enforcement watchdogs felt defeated. Few staff members felt good about the impact on public safety.

I made a spot arrest in my role as OD. Wally Karnitz had a Whitman County case named Hal. Wally's file said Hal had had trouble at his job and at a boarding house. Hal also had mental issues and got violent when he drank.

John Prideaux heard Hal was drinking in a tavern in downtown Spokane. It was late Friday afternoon and Wally was gone, so Prideaux asked me to find out if Hal was in fact drinking.

I decided to check the Blue Note Tavern first. If Hal wasn't there, I would not bother other staffers. With Hal's picture in my pocket, I drove to the Blue Note.

The tavern was dark as I stepped in. I was the only person in a suit, and all eyes turned to me. Hal was there and turned away quickly.

My back-up plan crumbled; if I went to the wall phone to call it in, he might run. So I walked to an empty stool next to him.

"Can I sit down?" I asked. "I'm Wally's friend. He's on vacation, but he's concerned about you."

Hal offered to buy me a beer.

"You'll get into trouble drinking," I said. "Bad things happen. You could be arrested and go to prison. Wally does not want that."

I asked him to walk to the jail with me to work things out. His head was down and his hands were on his glass.

To my surprise Hal said yes.

We walked into the warm air, past my car. Driving was not as safe as walking. Yes, he could run, but I would be safer if he got violent. We talked and walked past open stores. The traffic lights changed right on time, and we kept moving.

Hal's file said he could hurt citizens if he went into a zone; he was strong and hard to control. I was lucky he did not run, as I could have done little but wave goodbye.

A block from the station, Hal started telling me of a riot at the Medical Lake prison where he and others had taken hostages. I was getting nervous.

At the jail elevator, I pushed the up button.

Hal was quiet and he stayed quiet. At the booking desk the jailers gathered. Hal had been there before. Hal said, simply, "Goodbye."

I told him to take care, and that I would tell Wally that he had been no trouble.

In the elevator, I started down and saw, through the glass doors beyond the bars, that a fight had started at the booking desk. Hal was quiet no longer. Hal hated authority figures, but he had given me a pass because he wanted Wally's help.

Prideaux was surprised when I came back alone. He gave me the paperwork for Hal's arrest, so I wrote a detainer to hold Hal in custody. Wally would deliver it on Monday.

* * *

Bob Lizee, Bill Young, and Loran Lindseth, the agency's three regional supervisors, thought justice responses were driven by community values. For instance, stealing a cow in Okanogan was equivalent to bank robbery in Seattle. Conversely, a fight in a Seattle bar was assault, but in back-road bars it was viewed as folks letting off steam.

Lee Johnson was old school. He was retired and visited our office monthly. Lee had worked as a logger, a small town barber, a laborer at Grand Coulee Dam, a sheriff's deputy, and then a parole officer. In Lee's era there had been few rules; staff had freedom, and you satisfied your community by accepting that justice was inconsistent, and at times unjust, but so was life. He cared more about fairness than the rules, and he didn't negotiate.

Lee also had the gift of gab. He was not a deep thinker, but had common sense and was a verbal person, colorful and clear. People understood his blunt talk. Lee loved the woods and hunting, and visited my office when the hunters were busy.

I enjoyed his visits and hard-time stories of the Great Depression. He talked of horses and dumb loggers. Smart loggers learned after one pull that you do not walk behind a pulling team; slow learners walked in crap all day long, not learning from experience.

Lee believed that as long as there was no risk to the public everyone should get a second chance. He said not to make too much of the change in arrest policy, because he'd "rather interpret a Bible than write it." He felt an interpreter had options.

But with the improvement of technology, the Olympia office was able to do statewide comparisons. High-tech expansion allowed for standardized procedures and rules; interpretation was limited by terms such as "universal justice" or "best practices," and so power shifted away from the thirty-nine individual counties.

Lee valued one-on-one encounters, not systematic approaches. He felt threatened by far-reaching solutions. He wanted to see reasons behind outcomes.

* * *

My return to Spokane highlighted that surroundings count. In rural areas I had lacked treatment options and resources, but my clients couldn't hide. In the city my clients blended into crowds. I also found that though there were more treatment programs, not all were equal. Some programs claimed more success than they really had. They did this to survive in the referrals game. I visited each to see for myself, but the best gauge was the change in clients' behavior.

I looked for community follow-up. An addiction is not cured in a month—clients need ongoing help to create a healthy life. The stinking thinking that results in relapses is best reduced by tough love and caring discipline. Most important, clients must invest in their own program for it to be successful.

I was OD when Bob Banta said he had to go on a field visit. A client named Indian Jim was scheduled to report, and Bob could not wait for him.

"If Jim shows up, arrest him," Bob told me. "He's been drinking, and it must stop."

Bob left, time passed, and I forgot about Jim. Then I heard loud noises at our front desk.

A big Indian yelled, "I do not know Heffernan. I will see Bob!"

I stepped out and asked Jim to come down to my office.

"Bob asked me to talk to you about your drinking," I told him. "Bob said to place you under arrest."

Jim jumped up and ran. I called the sheriff's desk on the first floor near the elevator.

"Officer King," I said, "an Indian is flying down the stairs. Can you see he gets to jail?"

I filled out a detainer and took the elevator. Down the long hall, the jail door was closing. I followed the noise.

I found Jim at a booking desk and thanked officer King. He had caught Jim on the stairs with a hammerlock.

Jim said nasty things about getting me later.

"Banta would never arrest me," he said. "I won't forget it."

I placed the detainer and left. I called Banta and told him that Jim was under arrest and had made threats.

Monday I arrived at the office and, as I was unlocking our door, a voice behind me in the dark said, "Mr. Heffernan, Mr. Banta said I must apologize for what I said. I am sorry."

Jim's voice was a shock, given the threats. I was confused by the fact that he was out of jail so quickly.

"Thanks," I mumbled. "I'll tell Banta."

I visited Bob first thing when he arrived at work.

* * *

Bud Cox was the sheriff in Pend Oreille County from 1962 to 1974. He was low key, an expert in search and rescue. In World War II he had joined the navy to train as a deep-sea diver. After the war he was a town marshal in Ione, Washington, and worked the local mines.

One day in June 1965 I found Cox as angry as I had ever seen a man. He was not mad at me, but got upset while telling about an escape from his jail the prior year.

Two parolees from the coast, visiting friends in Newport, Washington, burglarized a drug store. Both were drunk, so they were arrested and held in the Newport jail. After their conviction, one used lead pencils and the power cord from a coffee pot to cut an upper jail window screen. The men then jumped from the window. Cox was angry because he had given them the coffee pot as an act of kindness.

Both men landed on Cox's boat, a pontoon boat that he had designed and built. He was proud of his stern-wheeler, and its pilothouse was crushed by the jump. No longer would his boat be a grand sight on the river.

Insurance did not cover the damage to his boat because it had occurred on county property. The men made a clean escape, and Cox wanted them in jail until they fixed his boat.

Months passed, his boat no longer near the jail. The escapees remained free for a year until they were arrested in Montana. Bud went on vacation when the escapees returned; he did not trust his temper. Eventually Cox's boat was fixed and back on the river.

* * *

Seldom do citizens in America face unrestrained power. The truth was that you could get others to do what you wanted by applying enough force. Yet force is not the foundation for positive changes that will ensure good behavior.

I used force only to prevent crime or bad things from happening. Some staffers carried guns and had unlisted phones and addresses. I did not. My first duty was to public safety. Probation and parole created confusion and conflict in citizens. Feelings ran high; crooks sought leniency, but victims believed that leniency punished communities and created crime.

Fear was useful for the lazy. With a little insight, it could evolve into self-control, even wisdom. If clients stayed positive and stable, they were less risk to others.

People who face fear eventually overcome their helplessness, since strong emotions do not stay around if they are not reinforced. The exception is dread, which lingers. Why dread but not fear?

Fear is a human defense—it says look, listen, be wary, and prepare for the unknown. Dread is a fear of a known entity.

Supervision deals with the unknown, specifically the risk of giving people second chances. Supervision success depends on the client's attitude, capacity, and performance. Most clients thought us petty for overreacting to technical violations.

How could I know if I struck an emotion evoking good behavior? I could not, so I allowed clients to make choices and I watched. I chased victory but tasted much failure.

Failures rippled through our office. I reviewed files and did extra home visits. We got smarter, and I was grateful to staffers who shared their failures and successes.

We were a silent service—if we did our job well, no one knew we existed. We offered options; courts and the parole board had the authority.

* * *

Citizens sought safety and our job was to reduce the risk of upsetting that safety. Two of our adages were: "If you can't do the time, don't do the crime," and "A life of crime is risky; wimps need not apply." Yet we were not the primary influence in offenders' lives.

The American vision was not of life in prison—parents did not raise children for that. Yet the phenomenon of gangs glorified crime, and bad choices upon bad choices had consequences over a lifetime. Youths exposed to bad influences ended up jailed and would always have a record.

Harmful social conditions exist and produce stress, broken families, negative peers, bad schools, drug abuse, and a lack of maturity. Today's society fosters substance abuse. Children face drug use early and that is a real crime because drugs destroy lives. Eighty percent of persons in prison have a history with drugs or alcohol abuse.

I saw little drug use by clients in 1965. One person used a prescription opiate and became addicted to the legal medication. He supported his habit by shoplifting, walking out of stores with arms full of stolen items.

A month after sentencing he came into my office to ask for prison. He wanted to get to a place where he would have no drug access. He got his wish, although I later found that drugs were in prisons. We did not cross paths again.

In 1966, the Spokane drug scene exploded. I had an inter-state parolee, Hank, who was my first contact with a street user. His thing was melting speed from inhalers in a spoon for injection. Hank had served time in Walla Walla and was now on parole from a state prison in Oregon. His transfer request said he would live at Spokane's Salvation Army Mission to avoid his old "friends" in Portland.

I found Hank living in a flophouse hotel on Main Street. He was unemployed. I decided to deny his transfer and return him to Oregon, but first I talked to the police, who knew Hank and his friends from go-go bars. None of his friends worked, but they all had money. The police asked me if I would wait, since Hank was under investigation.

I met with Hank and told him he had two weeks to find work or I would arrest him. Hank said he planned to return to Portland within the week. The next day he was in jail, charged with drug use, burglary, and counterfeiting. He had had no clue of the police's interest in him.

I soon learned that addicts live to feed their habit. Hooked on heroin or other hard drugs, their only goal was a fix. Practically overnight, Spokane saw more drug users and law enforcement became a new ballgame. Local police felt the impact first, then court dockets and jails were filled, and soon our office was involved.

* * *

The drugs in 1966 flowed from the social reforms that hit youths like a runaway freight train. Society could not restrain itself. Youths pretended to listen to older generations, but there were many peer forces at work. They often made bad choices in the absence of families. Parents worked to create a better life, unaware that addiction had taken over their child's life.

Flower children and hippies challenged the public view of drug use. They marched for civil rights and protested the war in Vietnam. In 1970, TV commercials sold cereal, cars, beer, coffee, and toothpaste. Cartoons babysat kids and fathers were preoccupied with televised sports.

TV had a powerful influence on passive living. Our society no longer seemed to value courage or hardship, or the lodges of the Elks, Moose, or Eagles. Nights were spent alone together with the television, and conversation was dull compared to the humor of Bob Hope.

We were frogs in a warming pot. No one noticed how we gave up special time together for nights before the tube. Racial equality, women's rights, and birth control brought individual freedom and work provided cash, and both had consequences. Family life decayed and strong marriages became less common. Within a decade, divorce became a fifty-fifty proposition.

Adults tried to relive their youth and avoided family duties while kids faced adult issues like aggression and dependency in broken homes. We coined the term latchkey children to describe the isolated life of kids. Families shaped offspring to their image. Cultural values shifted from hard work to entertainment, and youths paid the price.

History portends the future. We must look to history for clues as to our future behavior.

* * *

It was clear after working for a while that some humans caused high tensions by seeking success but finding failure. When a client failed, I failed. Stress affected staff members differently, especially when combined with their home and personal lives.

One natural condition for uncertainty was rumors and the tendency to play "what if" games. Playing rumor games in the corrections profession is like standing in a canoe in rough water—soon you get wet. It was a cyclical reality. Dark humor was a relief valve.

It was not surprising that office politics were alive and well as cases kept coming. I tried to keep out of the fray, for there was much to learn. In my third year of working and learning, I knew it would take more time to reach journeyman status. I was convinced it would take me five years. That said, I felt comfortable giving court input.

A sex offender transferred from Tacoma but his file was lost there. Larry lived in Spokane for three months without supervision. He needed my attention, as there were reports of attacks on girls. His address was in north Spokane.

I visited him the next day. He was not home and his sister was vague about his job. She was a single mom with young kids. She was clearly not happy.

"Larry must contact me tomorrow," I told her. "If I do not hear from him by four p.m., I will request his arrest. He was supposed to contact us when he arrived. I will not chase him, so the ball is in Larry's court."

I stopped at the police station, where detectives told me they were investigating several connected rapes. There were no eyewitnesses, as the victims were young, attacked from behind, with pillowcases put over their heads. All the victims said the attacker was a small man.

The rapes had occurred in homes near city parks. Police had no valid leads. A neighbor reported seeing a stranger at a bus stop wearing a coat of many colors. I told the detectives that Larry had been in Spokane for months.

Larry reported wearing a colorful coat. My first thought was, "Is it the bus stop coat?" He rode the bus and was unemployed. Larry was looking for a cook's job. He was small and in his late twenties. He could have passed for seventeen but his eyes showed that he was older. The jacket, the bus, and the free time bothered me.

"Larry, I want you to talk to city detectives," I told him. "You have been in town for months. I want you to know I work with police. This is only a visit." Larry knew I was serious and agreed.

"Our visit will take no more than an hour; I'll drive."

The drive downtown was quiet. Larry was not nervous as we entered the station elevator. Suddenly he stiffened, took off his coat, and looked me in the eye. His small smile gave me an eerie feeling. There was tension on his lips.

On the fifth floor, at the detectives' office, I introduced Larry. I had not met the detectives. They were formal and spoke with Larry because they had no other leads.

After greetings, I left. I did not want Larry playing off me.

I found a cup of coffee at the jail. They had great coffee—it was strong and free. I also wanted to learn what had happened to Hal.

I had not been to the jail since Hal's arrest, and I wanted to stay on good terms with Jim Reed, the chief jailer. I had heard that if Reed got upset, he would not open his jail door until Prideaux called him.

Reed reported that Hal had been no trouble when they booked him. Because he had not been drunk, Hal had not put up a major fight. I took a ribbing for ducking out.

A half hour and two cups of coffee later I went upstairs. Detectives talked in the hall as I walked up, unnoticed. One detective was shaking his head and saying, "I can't believe it."

Another detective, Gene, said, "Larry cleared five rapes and he is still talking."

He couldn't believe I had walked him into the station.

"We will not forget your help," he said.

Larry stayed for booking. I left my detainer. It was only noon.

With Larry's arrest, the police opened their doors to me. What I asked for, I got. I was in their club. Larry was held on rape and I denied his transfer. He pled guilty and went to prison. The Tacoma staff member who had lost his file had made a serious mistake.

* * *

Months later, the rumors about agency arrest policy came true. Staffers felt the loss, but clients still assumed we had arrest powers. The social workers relaxed and returned to their roots. Major fallout occurred in Seattle, Spokane, and Tacoma, as urban life attracted parolees searching for a new start.

In larger offices, specialist unit systems developed, e.g., court liaison, police liaison, and pre-sentencing. These specialties created a gap in developing rapport with clients, so supervision became less effective. With varied missions, functional fiefdoms evolved that focused on making process as important as public safety. Bad blood and friction were the natural result as entities narrowed their scope and views.

Fred Finsley saw the parole board as jurists who permitted, evaluated, and regulated. His views made him a lightning rod, but he was unconcerned and ignored politics, which was to his peril because he lived and worked in a political arena.

In 1966, upset Spokane staffers pushed back at Bob Lizee and John Prideaux. I avoided the entanglement; it was not useful. Lizee and Prideaux liked Finsley's leadership, but Fred quit about the time local staffers talked to Spokane's bench. Courts worried at the questions but did not receive a reply, as Olympia was busy creating policies.

A rebellion occurred, with the local court getting involved. They normally avoided involvement in agency policy. Police helped parole brothers.

I was not part of this debate, and I did not attend the meetings or get involved in any dialogue, and that worked for me. I felt no pressure.

I focused instead on getting a twenty-year-old to work, or getting a drunk to find help. The power to arrest was useful but distracting; it was a double-edged sword. Power of arrest might protect the public but it was also a cover for uninvolved staff. Personally I was focused on helping my clients become law-abiding citizens.

In 1967, Lizee talked of moving from the courthouse to larger offices. He wanted to relocate our office four blocks to the west, still on Broadway, and open offices in the valley and Colville.

Spokane's struggles never went critical, and in time tempers waned and we survived. Olympia staffers laid low. I was unaware at the time of plans to remove probation and parole field staff from the parole board and into the Department of Institutions.

* * *

Mike was a transfer from Jim Northrup.

"John, you're a social worker," Jim said. "You can help Mike better than I."

Mike was twenty going on twelve. He stood six feet tall and both his parents were on probation. In our first visit, I doubted Mike's chance of success. He seemed self-centered and he stuttered when upset or lying.

I suspected he used stuttering to manipulate people, so my plan was to ignore it and wait him out.

A high school dropout, Mike was married to a seventeen-year-old. They had a year-old baby. He worked for his parents in their café, washing dishes and cooking. He said they argued with him over his paying bills and got so upset that they fired him.

During his second visit Mike spent his time blaming both parents.

"Mike," I said, "that won't put food on your table. You need to work."

His file said his mother had been pregnant as a teenager. Mike's dad suspected that he was not Mike's father; for this and other reasons he ran around on Mike's mother. A family fight had led to bad checks, and those checks caused their probation.

Mike manipulated until he got his way, a skill he learned from his parents. His style was unhelpful on report days. I was brief with him—I wanted an address, job, income, and status of bills. I looked for anomalies, fuzzy facts, or nervous replies that suggested I should make a home visit.

His next report day, Mike was still not working. He said he might return to work at the café the following week. His wife's folks were paying rent and utilities.

He stuttered all meeting and I got no answers.

Mike got upset when I said, "I'll see you Monday, and each Monday, until you work. You share your efforts every week." Mike begged, but I remained firm.

Days later Mike was shot in the butt during a burglary. He had broken into a Second Avenue hardware store. A silent alarm had alerted police and Mike was inside when police arrived. He dropped his loot and ran. The police ordered him to stop, but he ignored them and was shot while climbing a fence. The shot had been intended as a warning.

Mike felt lucky not to have any serious injuries. He grew up a little after the impact as his limp reminded him to stay straight. His sentence was prison.

Mike felt that someone was looking after him. He believed he had a future. On wood crutches, he promised me he would learn a trade and stay out of trouble.

Months later, Mike returned as an apprentice welder and high school graduate. He spoke slower. He had grown up and wanted to be a good husband and father. He had changed.

* * *

In early 1966 I started using a sales technique with clients. I tried to get their investment early to build on success. I saw more options once I respected clients' choices.

A happy customer reinvests, but still it takes time to reverse bad habits. I did not ask for too much. There is no such thing as a bad sale unless it is too costly. Steve was an example of this. Steve was married with a young son and worked as a painter.

At our first meeting, Steve looked me in the eye and lied. He and his friends had drunk at a tavern on Illinois Avenue until it closed. Later they returned to take beer and meat.

Steve knew the owner had been selling bootleg meat behind his bar and would not report a theft. But the tavern's alarm went off when they entered. They left just before police arrived and found beer and meat missing. When Steve tried to sell his meat to a Hillyard grocer he was in jail within hours. All Steve's friends were safely home.

Police knew others were involved, but Steve refused to rat on his friends.

I saw him when he was released on bond. He had pled guilty to burglary. I did his pre-sentence report, and he was nervous because he had a juvenile record.

Steve was loyal but not strong; he was easily led, which was his problem. If he had avoided bad friends, he would likely have stayed out of trouble.

I stressed that punishment was a long road, and his silence would make it longer. I told him his friends were sitting in bars drinking beer. I said if he were serious about going back to his family he would use this chance to get leniency for himself.

By our third visit Steve had seen the inside of prison. I heard stress in his voice. Finally he cried uncle and gave up his friends for probation. He did not want to risk an angry judge. He feared prison.

Soon I saw the repercussions for Steve. He was labeled a snitch, and he lost his job as crew members refused to work with him. One accomplice was his brother-in-law, and fingering him cost Steve his marriage.

Steve moved to Yakima because he received death threats. In Yakima he violated probation by drinking in bars and was sentenced to the reformatory.

In the reformatory, playing softball, he was about to bat when a blow to the back of his head nearly killed him.

When I heard of the snitch attack I realized I had not put my customer first as a good salesman always does. I ran into Steve later and he did not recognize me. Never again did I put a client under such pressure. I decided that if there were risks to take, I should take them myself.

* * *

My priorities were always public safety, stopping crime, and being a change agent, but I had no special gifts. My main chores were to identify trends and provide feedback to clients.

My product was freedom, and to make a sale I discerned how clients viewed or valued their freedom. Humans acquire their values young, but this is not to say offenders could not reform.

My sales experience had started when I worked part-time as a bookkeeper for Standard Equipment in 1961. I ran the shop when the owner, Ivan, was gone. I saw many salesmen, but one stood out. He sold no-name equipment and his prices were high, yet he outsold all the others.

I asked him, “Chuck, how do you do it?”

He smiled and pulled out a little book listing customers, their wives' and children's names, and their hobbies. Chuck explained that he reviewed his book before a meeting so he could ask questions like "How was Nancy's birthday party?"

Chuck sold himself before he sold his product. It was a valuable lesson.

* * *

One prominent symbol of justice is the blind woman with scales for fairness. Yet crime is intrinsically unfair, so there is no possible valid repayment to victims.

Life itself is seldom fair. I shook my head once when I heard of a 125-year prison sentence. Do we think an inmate will live that long? Big numbers are sometimes as close to closure as the public can get.

People experience prison differently. Some find it a relief; to others it is hell. It depends on each person's ability to adjust. Inmates must learn to live a day at a time. No one escapes the fear, boredom, or anger at oneself and at prison conditions.

The only escape is in the mind, and many inmates grow numb. Endless days cease to have meaning, which blunts the value of long sentences as a deterrent to crime. Criminals never expect to be arrested, so the threat of a long prison term is inherently ineffective.

A useful sentence would adjust to an inmate's prison behavior, since conduct demonstrates evolving habits. Testing an offender's ability to change and retesting often would save a lot of money.

To make probation and parole work, citizens must demand that staff work with clients to change inmates' perspectives.

I demanded that clients pay restitution, I wanted to know their friends, and I insisted that they comply with probation rules. Most clients followed the rules—the vast majority bumped their noses a couple of times and then adjusted to supervision. Only about 20 percent played games and had to face tough choices.

My job was to keep them focused on the reality that they had something to prove to regain their full freedom.

* * *

The debate over what spawns crime is unending. The impetuses for crime are the seven sins: fear, anger, guilt, lust, and greed. These are all hurtful acts. Forgiveness is uplifting.

Human nature plays a part in crime, yet acts are only illegal if authorities define them as such. Laws express our culture's values through elected officials who write rules to promote the common good.

Society creates laws to parallel violations of moral codes, such as greed (fraud), lust (rape), stealing (burglary), and drunkenness (DUI). When citizens declare specific acts illegal, there is likely an underlying religious declaration of immorality.

Yet the legal code does not always mirror the moral code. For example, a buyer beware philosophy in marketplaces allows big businesses to reap wild profits. Outrage against those profits is often a moral argument, but the law does not declare profits illegal. Lobbyists argue to keep it that way, no matter the public outcry.

A legal issue arose when I first visited Eastern State Hospital (ESH). Criminally insane clients were added to my caseload, their files over an inch thick. These patients were found not guilty of crimes due to mental illness.

Eastern State Hospital was a self-contained hospital on land between Medical Lake and West Medical Lake. Patients could spend years in the wards, but since the mid-sixties, drug therapy allowed patients to return home if they were stabilized on medication. I knew little about mental illness, so I questioned that release policy.

The hospital buildings were massive, and a strange feeling came over me as I signed in. Bob, a counselor, walked me through locked doors into ward after ward. Vaulted 1930s ceilings made me feel small; it was surreal. The constant chatter of patients raised the hair on my neck. Yelling and shouting added to the confusion as patients talked to air, argued with plants, or stared vacantly.

Each ward was filled to capacity. I met clients who were not aware of time or space. I suspected that Bob purposely gave the grand tour so he could educate me.

Our last ward was Harry's. Harry seemed like a wild man with his spastic motions and unfocused eyes. His unkempt clothes and wild hair gave him the look of a mad professor.

Bob asked if Harry could be granted a home visit, and I shook my head no way.

"That action needs a judge's okay," I said. "His parents would need to agree."

A sly look crossed Harry's face at the mention of his parents.

When we left the ward, I told Bob I did not appreciate his home visit question.

The next day, Harry's parents were in my office. They were salt of the earth folk, Norman Rockwell types. They showed up every week. I put them off for a month, but by the sixth visit they had worn me down.

We talked, and I forgot about Harry's wild hair and eyes. I told them I would talk to the judge.

To my surprise the judge approved a short furlough. I suddenly saw myself trapped without options. I wondered why I requested the furlough if I did not support it. I left chambers shaking my head. I decided to keep my mouth shut. Harry would be on a short leash. "How do I get into these messes?" I thought.

Ten days later reality arrived. Harry and his parents walked in, and Harry looked worse than I remembered. He had a sly look pasted on his face, and his eyes wandered as he tried to act normal. His family was happy to have the weekend together.

Midday, Harry called me and said, "My father had a heart attack at Safeway on Sprague."

I had been expecting a call from the police or a neighbor, but not this call.

I told Harry I would come pick him up, but he had called an ambulance and did not want to leave his mother.

"Phone me when your dad is stable," I told him.

At six p.m. he called and said, "I'll take Mother home and cook her dinner." His dad was in recovery. Caught off guard, I agreed to let him stay home to help. He was scheduled to report to Eastern State Hospital on Monday.

Hospital staff contacted the court for a furlough extension to allow Harry to stay at home. I saw Harry weekly and with each visit he seemed more alert, more normal. He even combed his hair.

Still, his crime had been serious. He had hit a ten-year-old girl in the head with a rock. Police assumed sexual interests, yet he was declared not guilty due to insanity. The judge had not wanted to risk a second attack, so Harry was taken to ESH.

After a month at home, Harry returned to the hospital, but staff refused to admit him. I reminded them that Harry was legally committed and that only a judge could change Harry's status; that was not likely to happen in the near term.

Harry was readmitted, but the staff went on a psychiatric test crusade. Harry scored normal each time and again they recommended release.

His judge said not yet, but granted a long furlough. I was to see Harry weekly for six months, and then he would be re-evaluated. Harry had to work and tell his employer about his crime so they could monitor him, and he also had to live at home.

I felt that his father's heart attack had shocked Harry, altering how he saw himself and how others saw him. His mental illness appeared to be in full remission. Harry transformed, his trial period went smoothly, and he was sentenced to ten years on supervision. I never had any trouble with him.

* * *

My co-workers were either proactive or reactive. I was proactive because I felt citizens expected us to be engaged. I tried hard to influence clients to comply with rules and conditions.

If clients failed to comply, they returned to court. I pushed for good results, but I experienced some failures and with each came a lesson. I listened more to assess clients' strengths or weaknesses, to find help or treatment options.

I coached clients to find resources and make good choices. My interview skills improved through interaction. It took practice and more practice to find success.

An Alcoholics Anonymous sponsor told me the old saying, "You can lead a horse to water, but you can't make him drink." I could not ensure good results, only work hard to make them happen. Life is not a jigsaw puzzle with a single solution.

So I listened and encouraged. I informed, motivated, or investigated, but I did not instruct. I felt people must make their own choices, and if I saw a positive one I supported it. I tried to sell clients on the idea that their success was worth whatever effort it required.

Epiphanies occurred, and with each revelation my work grew easier. I had no fountain of truth. I did not play catch-up with clients; rather I believed that small investments over time would allow their commitment to freedom to grow.

Yet I sometimes struggled as a coach. My own bad habits died hard, and at times I could not keep quiet. When this happened I tried harder in the next interview. The most difficult person to manage was myself.

Having problems is part of life, and problems exist, just like beauty, in the eye of the beholder. I did not try to understand or assume to tell someone what he or she was thinking. Life is made up of changes, and sometimes I had to reset my goals daily.

Changing a habit is never easy. Newton's law of motion applies with habits—things in motion tend to stay in motion until stopped by an equal and opposite force. With that in mind, small goals are better and more reachable.

* * *

I learned a lesson from a client, a young man from Yakima named Frank. His only family was a son and a grandmother from the Flathead tribe. His grandmother helped Frank raise his son. Frank's ex-wife had been a runaway teenager in Seattle. Frank's father was a farm worker, his mother a tribal member. Both of his parents were alcoholics who died young.

Frank's grandmother moved to Spokane to keep Frank from his drinking friends. He was a quiet man, a high school dropout on probation for bad checks.

His grandma took my side. Frank respected his grandmother, so Frank started attending high school and hoped to work construction to make his grandma proud; he did right and graduated high school. Afterward, his grandmother died. Frank avoided drinking at her funeral in Yakima and returned to Spokane. An aunt, his mother's sister, took Frank's son with her to the reservation in Montana.

Frank worried for his son, but stayed in Spokane to find a job. He got a job that required steel-toed work boots, which he did not have. The boots cost $100. I had money in my pocket from payday, so I loaned Frank money for the boots. That was the last I saw of him. Instead of boots he bought a bus ticket to Canada. That lesson cost me $100, but I felt good about it. I felt that I had connected with Frank.

* * *

My role model for selling was the door-to-door salesman on a buyer's doorstep, except, with a badge, no one kicked me off the porch. I hoped a buyer—my client—would invest, see the result, and invest more. I appealed to greed, pride, or self-interest. My approach was driven by each client's interest or ability to pay.

Once, at coffee, Dave Schafer shared an insight. He said there were three categories of crooks: the situational, the habitual, and the adaptive.

The situational criminal was an average person who made a bad choice and knew it as soon as he or she was arrested. He will be no trouble since no external force drove his behavior.

Situational offenders accepted community values. They were embarrassed by their crime, and if I offered an option they took it. Their arrest and write-up in the newspaper was enough shame.

Habitual criminals were addicted to drugs, alcohol, sex, greed, bad friends, or golf. Their addiction controlled their motives; all they wanted was their next fix. Making a sale to habitual criminals meant I first had to get past their addiction, so addiction treatment was necessary.

I saw few drug addicts in 1966; alcohol abuse was the more common issue. Another was having bad influences and associates.

Unresolved anger could lead to fights or bad money-handling skills to bad checks. Greed was a main factor in fraud, forgery, and theft.

Sexual offenders target vulnerable people because they want control. The nature of a sex crime requires a secret life. Sex offenders live in denial and appear at first blush to be impossible to control. Yet, like everyone who hurts others, sex offenders can and do change over time.

Adaptive crooks are professionals who live in a culture that reinforces a criminal lifestyle. They tend to cooperate because they do not worry. Their loss of freedom is a cost of business, and they believe straight people are goofy.

With adaptive criminals I tried but got no sale; it was against their code. I did not see many mob people, gang members, or psychopaths.

* * *

In April 1966 I was promoted to run the Walla Walla office, which was a one-man office. Kathy and I were to be married in early October. My promotion ensured my paycheck would pay our bills without Kathy working outside our home.

Our plan was to spend two years in Walla Walla, then transfer back to Spokane. I moved to a temporary rental apartment in May; we would select our home once Kathy arrived. Prior to the transfer I oversaw two pre-sentence investigations, both of them messy: the Pride Castle drug case.

A man named Bob and his wife, Ann, pled guilty to drug use and lewd living. They were flower children from California and lived in an open marriage. The newspapers detailed their lifestyle on the front page in bold print. It was a circus. Talk of sex offended everyone in the valley, even those with no religion.

The reports detailed all-night parties. A seventeen-year-old boy and two eighteen-year-old girls were involved with Ann and Bob, who were in their mid-twenties. The youths had lived on the road since age fourteen.

The mess was mine to deal with, and after looking into it I found more smoke than fire. The marijuana case was weak—it was not clear who bought what or when. The boy and two girls had juvenile records. The media called for harsh sentences to send a juvenile records. The media called for harsh sentences to send a message and return God to the valley.

I suggested county jail for Bob and Ann, not prison. Soon they were transferred to California. When my reports were done I left town for Walla Walla.

Walla Walla
1966–1969

Walla Walla was a step back in time. I arrived in town after snowmelt runoff and spring floods had closed Highway 12. Mill Creek had gone over its banks with water flowing from the hills and nearby Blue Mountains. Mill Creek was normally a lazy creek, but that flooding caused a detour for a month.

My office was on the fourth floor of the five-story brick Drumheller Building. The first floor held a hardware store. The offices on the upper floors had large bay windows.

I got my office keys from Bob Kastama at Pete's Broiler Café a block up the street. John Prideaux joined us and showed me around, as Kastama was leaving on vacation. Kastama had been promoted but was not leaving town. His new job was on the pre-parole desk at the Washington State Penitentiary (WSP). John had worked in town before Bob and knew everyone. We did the rounds of introductions with local officials.

The Walla Walla County Prosecuting Attorney's Office and a number of attorneys and accountants rented space on my floor. Wood and glass walls, circa 1930, framed wide halls.

A gray-haired, properly dressed woman ran our elevator and monitored my visitors. Just down the hall from my office was a county prosecutor whose receptionist answered my phone when I went out.

Alex Dietz, captain of the city police, asked me to join the morning coffee group at a corner café. I liked his offer.

The Walla Walla County Sheriff's Office is where I met Sheriff Art Klundt. Art was tall and well dressed. He had a square chin, a full head of gray hair, and a deep voice.

Art was one of the few people I met that day who talked about the penitentiary; he had little positive to say. He seemed to think that if the penitentiary did not exist, he would have no trouble. His principal complaint was state prisoners, and he connected that problem with state staff. I kept quiet and listened to John and Art banter.

"Don't take Art seriously," John suggested. "You can work with him or around him."

Still, after meeting Art, I knew life would get interesting down the road.

The sheriff's office was next door to the courthouse. There I met Judges Tuttle and Bradford, who were both to start summer break in June. While on break, they would only have court once a week, on Wednesdays. The summer schedule would continue until mid-September.

John was friendly with the judges; his wife, Ann, worked for a retired judge. Judge Bradford had attended law school at Gonzaga. Both Bradford and Tuttle had liked Bob Kastama's work.

After lunch it was time for John to leave for Spokane. He would visit routinely, and said I could call Bob if I had issues. But in reality Bob and I lived in separate worlds. I worked downtown and would travel to outlying counties, while Bob would stay at the penitentiary.

* * *

I was the lone staffer doing parole and probation work in the shadow of the Washington State Penitentiary. Nicknamed the Hill, the WSP sat on a rise to the northwest, looming day and night. Its lights lit up the night sky. With its limited town contacts, the Hill might as well have existed on another planet.

The WSP had opened in 1887, in territorial days, as a replacement for the 1874 territorial prison at Seatco, Washington. In 1908, the Washington State Reformatory opened at Monroe. In 1964, the Washington Corrections Center opened at Shelton.

Historically, female prisoners had been held at the WSP in quarters outside the walls, but in 1970 female prisoners were moved to the Washington Corrections Center for Women at Gig Harbor.

People in Walla Walla had a blind spot for the penitentiary's existence even as its silhouette dominated sunsets. Parole board policy ensured that only local inmates were paroled into Walla Walla County because inmates' families often moved to town, and that would increase the city's population without restriction.

I could see the prison from downtown, but my focus was on the free world. My objective was to settle in as the local probation and parole officer; I did not ask a lot of big-picture questions.

I fell into my routine quickly in the Drumheller Building. My office was across from the elevator and opened at eight o'clock, as did the prosecutor's office. The other offices opened at nine. I left daily to pick up my mail four blocks away.

I stopped at the corner café for coffee with police and to trade information. I caught up on the news and gossip. We played games to determine who would pay for coffee.

I rented a cheap, good-sized apartment near Whitman College. In July I found out why it was cheap—the heat rose and it stayed hot into the evenings. The space only cooled if I left windows open and a breeze arrived. I worked late to avoid the heat and ate dinner in local cafés.

My office stayed cool on hot days. Still, when Kathy joined me, we looked for an air-conditioned apartment, as cool air was necessary. We rented an apartment in a townhouse on Palouse Street a few blocks from downtown.

Air conditioning made quite a difference. Our apartment had two bedrooms, two bathrooms, a living room, a kitchen, and a breakfast area. We were one of eight units, and each had a back yard and patio.

On weekends we walked and window-shopped, as money was short. Walking for ice cream cones was a big outing.

In 1966, the fall Washington Correctional Association (WCA) conference was in Walla Walla. We were on our honeymoon at the time. When I returned I heard it had been a wild conference, and there were rumors of transferring our agency to the Department of Institutions.

At morning coffee, no one talked about the penitentiary even as they talked about the conference.

Courthouse halls were dark in the summer. Prosecutors in small rural counties were part-time, with private practices and offices. Only the clerk's office stayed open over the summer. Judges heard motions or signed court papers on Wednesdays, so I did have some visit time.

Judge Jordan sat on the Garfield County bench in Pomeroy, the Columbia County court in Dayton, and the Asotin County bench in Asotin. Jordan was a fly angler and had a favorite creek in Columbia County.

The Columbia County Sheriff called in late summer to say he had arrested two car thieves near Starbuck, Washington. They had pled guilty and received a year in prison. That term was suspended for a sundown parole to Oregon.

I saw the court orders and told court officials the sentence was not legal; Washington law required prison sentences to carry the maximum term, which was ten years for auto theft. Courts could defer terms and grant conditional probation if they wished.

Judge Jordan, who had been fishing on Patti Creek, returned to court and issued a proper sentence with sundown probation, so the two car thieves left for Oregon. It turned out that a part-time prosecutor had not read the Revised Code of Washington (RCW).

Most of summer was quiet with the courts closed, and I used the time to learn my cases. I also made contacts with officials in neighboring counties. I visited with my notebook, and I wrote brief clips on each person for future reference.

The majority of my clients, sixty-five, lived in Walla Walla. I spent four days per week in town. My travel day was on Wednesday, and I had fifteen total cases in three small counties. Highway 12 cut over rolling hills. I arrived in Waitsburg or Dayton at eight and drove to Pomeroy and then to Clarkston. My return trip was nonstop. Every other week I stayed a night in Clarkston and returned the next morning.

One local challenge in Walla Walla was finding employment for my clients. Waitsburg and Dayton had canneries and hired seasonal workers to process asparagus, fruit, and peas. After harvest was over, work slowed to a crawl, except the years when dam work created pockets of highly paid jobs building dams, railroads, or bridges.

My plan was to get ahead of the job cycle in March, when service jobs opened briefly. I pushed my clients to take service jobs, but most clients did not realize that probation success and work were closely related.

I met with employment security to find out about spring openings in April; after that there would be no new jobs until late August when harvest would start.

In late summer, as harvest grew near, the town awoke. The courthouse lights turned on and courts were back in session. Motels filled with sellers and buyers. Labor camps opened in Dayton and Waitsburg, and there were crowds in shops and on street corners. Car dealerships had customers again.

Planning helped ease the troubles of this boom and bust job cycle. In winter, equipment needed painting or repairs. Planting time was a good opportunity for seasonal work. My caseload violation rates dropped as I got better at finding jobs.

* * *

I was impressed with Walla Walla. It was well kept and its citizens had pride in their town. Storeowners washed their sidewalks daily. Visitors were drawn to historic sites, as Walla Walla was the first white settlement in the Washington Territory.

More millionaires per capita lived in Walla Walla than any other town in the Pacific Northwest, yet folks did not show off. They quietly kept up their historic homes, parks, and old buildings. Old families valued their reputations. I supervised a few old guard members, and their files were kept sealed in the clerk's office. I had to sign out files, which stayed at the courthouse.

Local leadership was slow to adapt to changes because of the town's rural nature. People feared changing their routines. Food companies, colleges, the penitentiary, even scientific folks had to adapt to the values of the rural community made up largely of farming families.

A few families were wealthy, and their children were unlikely to earn an income that equaled their future inheritance. This created an upside-down existence for rich kids—they avoided finding a profession and simply waited to get rich.

Mixed in with the rich families were old-line pioneer families who had lost their wealth but held onto their name and honor. Their status as established families was important, and they considered anyone who arrived after 1900 a newcomer.

Kathy joined a newcomers club that met weekly and had a monthly session for couples. The other families in our townhouse were members.

The husbands of the wives in the club were engineers, sales representatives, car dealers, state employees, or business managers. Meetings were fun social affairs. Kathy's involvement got her out of the apartment and kept her busy with coffee meetings, tea times, and lunches.

My daily routine was solitary. I sometimes went weeks without seeing visitors. It crossed my mind that no one cared that I was at work. There was not even any gossip.

But things picked up in a hurry in July 1967 when, without fanfare, Probation and Parole Field Services was transferred to the Department of Institutions.

* * *

There had been vague rumors in the past, but I had not been aware the move was coming. I felt blindsided. Once a small outfit, we were now a division within a much larger agency. At first there were few changes beyond new letterhead and more training, but I did miss coffee visits to sort out the changes.

The move put an end to struggles between field service leadership and the parole board. Going forward we would have agency leadership with a background in prison work. At a regional meeting I learned that Fred Finsley was gone. Most staff members were upbeat. The new parole board chairman, Bruce Johnson, worked more closely with staff, and many of the historic fights vanished.

I heard positive comments. The common view was that we could be a seamless system from prison to parole. "Brothers on the

Hill" was a new catch phrase. To be seamless, parole board members would have to be judicial and stay at arm's length.

Probation and parole was no longer in the spotlight. Some staffers said we had lost access to the governor. Others said we could be professional in the absence of political hacks. Headquarters was happy and optimistic about our in-house assets and likely pay raises.

The transfer to the Department of Institutions did not affect me much. I still worked with the courts and increasingly attended pre-parole sessions. We did get a pay raise. Surprisingly, Finsley's changes stuck because the new leadership liked operational standards.

We saw a new, formalized board hearing process, and it altered basic supervision. Submitting reports for hearings was no longer enough for attorneys, since they could not cross-examine reports. Probation and parole officers had to attend hearings in person. Hearings became more complicated as witnesses testified before the board.

Staff spent more time handling paperwork and logistics, so we had less time to do fieldwork. The prison population was growing, driven by a new drug culture. Overcrowded prisons and larger caseloads distracted us from seeing the Department of Social and Health Services (DSHS) on the horizon.

We had no idea more change was about to occur with our agency.

* * *

The WSP was the flagship of punishment in Washington and inmates lived in harsh conditions. During my time in Walla Walla the Hill was relatively quiet. The corrections center in Shelton had drawn down the inmate population and female inmates had been transferred to Gig Harbor, which created minimum-security space for farm workers and trustees. Some cells were converted for school and recreation use.

I seldom visited the Hill. When I did, I saw Warden Bobby Rhay, who had worked on the Hill for twenty years. I was the backup for pre-parole reports and handled those duties when Kastama was out of town.

If I had to visit the Hill I tried to get in and get out quickly. The air felt weird and made me uncomfortable. In 1964 I had visited to give pre-parole classes on agency rules and parolee obligations. Now, in 1967, I visited much more often.

John Prideaux had introduced me to Warden Rhay in 1966 when we toured the WSP. Rhay showed us the sally port where he had once stopped an escape by grabbing a pistol and firing at the escapee; the bullet was still lodged in the ceiling.

On the tour we had climbed iron stairs to a walkway on the nineteen-foot wall overlooking more than twenty acres. Later we walked through steel doors into the prison courtyard. I felt odd as the door closed behind us. We also toured the eight wings of housing and the hospital. A tower guard followed us the whole time, his rifle ready.

Warden Rhay was on the county fair board. His interest was horses. He kept a low profile, but there was no doubt he ran the Hill.

Parole Board Chairman Bruce Johnson called me if he had bad news, or if a request from Rhay was denied. I no longer worked for the board, but I carried messages out of habit.

When I delivered Johnson's messages, Rhay sometimes exploded and then ignored the message. Rhay's raw anger was frightening; he was not a patient man. When Rhay made a decision he did not look back.

Town folk heard rumors, but never saw the angry forces Rhay contained. His pot simmered but never boiled over. Rhay's replies were swift. Inmates and staff were either beholden to him or in fear of him. An argument with Rhay meant isolation for prisoners. A staff mistake meant termination. Tension ran high for both the keepers and the kept. Everyone counted the days to release or retirement.

But on the Hill clocks ticked a bit slower. It was a hard place with hard rules. A nineteen-foot-high wall marked by armed towers surrounded the twenty-eight buildings. One covered breezeway would become known as Blood Alley. The Hill had seen two major riots in the 1950s and also a devastating fire. I avoided trips to the Hill as I would avoid a wounded wild animal.

Down the road, kids played in front yards and folks lived with hope. The Hill kept angry, bad, and violent people off the main streets of Washington State, but citizens were not aware of the raw vengeance inside the penitentiary.

* * *

Locals mostly ignored the Hill, but had strong views on inmates, their families, and the WSP staff. Children were ridiculed if they had a relative on the Hill. It was guilt by association.

We all pay for prisons but turn a blind eye to why they grow. If a criminal is not locked up, citizens question if the justice system is working. It is an emotional response, not a call for real solutions.

Some citizens question how much prison time is useful, asking what the proper punishment for a bad crime is. Is it triple the life sentence, or is it death? Moreover, what kind of punishment will deter lesser crimes? Is it maiming, shaming, jailing, redirecting, banishing, or perhaps educating?

Banishment had long been an accepted way to deal with criminals. Adam and Eve were banished from the Garden of Eden as their punishment. God disciplined Cain for Abel's death by rejection.

In antiquity, banishment was serious; folks had to have the support of others to survive. Banishment even helped push civilization around the world—English debtor's prisons and penal colonies swelled the populations of America and Australia. Crooks run out of eastern towns built and shaped the American West. The French used Devil's Island to punish evildoers. By the Civil War era, states looked to prisoners for hard labor.

Today, taxpayers pay to banish criminals to prisons and the cost is incredibly high. We ignore options that provide better outcomes even though one in seven people knows an incarcerated person.

Prison life often shocks ordinary citizens when they see the fear, anger, guilt, loneliness, and loss of humanity that pervade the prison system. Without staff to control cellblocks they become combat zones.

Fear is, in my mind, the obvious metaphor for the blood denied to Shylock in *The Merchant of Venice.* Shylock is allowed a pound of Antonio's flesh but no blood, and he takes nothing at all for fear of spilling one drop of blood. Today a person is sentenced to an amount of time, yet we also extract fear in unsafe prison conditions. The state has a duty to ensure safety after taking away liberty.

My question is, can we do better?

* * *

Sheriff Art Klundt's county jail had not been built for long-term housing. To keep costs down, Klundt had a jailer and his wife living in an apartment above the jail. The space was rent-free in exchange for cooking and night security. Klundt also cut costs by having trustees clean, cut lawns, and wash cars. His only real costs were the prisoners' three meals a day.

State inmates from the Hill were housed for court days in the county jail, where high-security space was precious.

In 1967 the live-in jailer told me about an escape attempt that had happened before my arrival.

The escape was unsuccessful, but a trustee, Elize, said he had helped. The jailer said that was not true.

The truth was that Elize had fallen ill. After a checkup a jail doctor had told Elize that it was cancer causing his stomach pains.

Elize was an alcoholic who had no job, no friends, and no insurance. The jailer had told Elize that on the Hill the state covered medical bills. So Elize pled guilty to assisting an escape in order to get medical care.

Once on the Hill, a state doctor told Elize there was no cancer; he simply had an ulcer. The doctor told him that if he stopped drinking heavily and drank milk instead, he would be fine. The jailer told me that that was two years ago.

"Can you help Elize?" he asked me. The board would not parole Elize without a plan, and the jailer would not write a report because he feared losing his job.

"Without a statement," I said, "I can do nothing."

* * *

The Hill brought both wealth and trouble to town. There were the WSP jobs, but the state did not always pay the county jail's invoices on time, and there were disputes over the jail's costs. As a state employee, I often heard Art's complaints.

"My jail is my jail," he said. "It is not for state use." He stopped allowing me to keep clients in his jail.

Art turned red when he was serious. I had not met a Klundt type—I had never had to worry about jail access before. Visits to Art's office were brief, and I left shaking my head.

His staffers, Liebmann and Ray, were helpful except when it came to jail access. "Talk to Art," they said.

I knew his answer would be no.

I worked around the issue and hoped the conflict would make me better somehow, but the problem stayed front and center. It caused me to find alternatives to jail. I knew, in time, a test would come. Then I would make my decision and live with it.

A female client named Mary, who had been arrested for shoplifting, was the test. Linda Chapman wrote a report to Judge Tuttle, and I arrested Mary at the city jail after her shoplifting term ended and took her to the county jail.

But Klundt would not admit Mary. She had health issues and medical bills were likely, including the cost of posting a deputy at the hospital.

Without debate, I handed Klundt my detainer. "Do what you like and tell it to Judge Tuttle. I brought her to jail. You tell Tuttle why she is not in court."

Art turned black. He kept Mary and never again spoke of holding cases. For a while he and his staff did not talk to me; if I entered, staff suddenly got busy and avoided eye contact. If a deputy met with me it was not at the office—no one wanted to be on Art's black list.

* * *

In spring 1968 a youth named Dan showed up with his parents. Dan had pled guilty to auto theft and was granted probation without a pre-sentence hearing because Judge Bradford was clearing his docket for June recess. Dan and his parents visited me prior to Deputy Prosecutor Johnson sharing Dan's file with me.

Dan's parents tried to keep him calm, but Dan was eighteen and angry after his plea. He wanted me to retry his case.

"That is not how it works," I told him.

He said his parents had talked him into a plea, and I listened for a minute. Right after the plea was not a good time to meet, as Dan almost talked himself into jail. I needed facts before I could make a decision, and I thought Dan would settle down over the weekend.

I was wrong. Dan arrived on Monday in a foul mood. He felt screwed over and said so, sitting red-faced on the edge of his chair, leaning over my desk.

I looked Dan in the eye and said, "I'm not your daddy. If you spend a month in jail, that won't give me heartburn. You'll get no water from this dry well."

I was about to pull out handcuffs, but his expression changed.

"Why is life unfair?" I asked him. "Why are you screwed?"

I got ten minutes of why life was unfair.

When he ran out of steam I said, "What will make your world right, Dan?"

He immediately said, "A good job with good pay."

He was a high school dropout, with no job skills I knew of. "What are good wages?" I asked him.

He said, "Ten dollars an hour."

I called his bluff and phoned the local Employment Security Department office. I gave them Dan's history and asked if they had work for him.

I expected to hear $1.50 per hour. Instead they said there was work at Wells Dam on a railroad bridge near Central Ferry. It paid $14 per hour traveling and $27 on the iron.

I passed it on to Dan and he grinned.

"Do you have boots and a hard hat?" I asked Dan.

"Yes," he said. "I'll take it."

He was to be at the employment office at 6 a.m. on Monday.

Two days after his job started, Dan was waiting for me as I exited the elevator. The Wells Dam bridge was a hundred feet above the water. He had frozen on the high iron and had to be carried off by a supervisor. Dan decided that wages were not vital, and told me he would be no trouble at all. He took a job at a gas station and enrolled in summer school.

Dan finished high school and went to auto mechanic class. He never was any trouble. Years later, when I was in town for a meeting, Dan pumped my gas. By that point he owned the station. He did not recognize me, as with age I got better looking. Dan smiled as he checked my oil.

"Looks like it's going to be a hot day," he said.

Dan had probably forgotten his instant rehabilitation a hundred feet above the Snake River.

* * *

The 1968 WCA conference was in Vancouver, Washington. I put faces to names I'd heard and mingled with power brokers. I was impressed with one speaker in particular, Dr. David Glazer. Glazer had written *Reality Therapy* and spoke on why people select a lifestyle. It sounded like common sense to me.

He spoke clearly, saying things I believed but had never expressed. Glazer's theme hit home; he said, "Don't assume others are where you want them to be. Rather, start from where they are."

His advice was fundamental to supervision and good teaching. Supervision done properly empowers people and allows them to pursue self-interests, improve income, or grow stronger ties with family or friends. To be effective, I had to listen when others stated their beliefs. I needed to value clients beyond their complicity to our process. I was already using Glazer's ideas as my supervision template, but he gave me a road map.

From Glazer I realized that income is critical, as we live in a materialistic culture. Work takes up a third of a person's life and in turn puts food on the table. Earning power determines lifestyle, grants social status, establishes identity, and increases options.

Earning levels predict future conduct, sex crimes excluded. Work is visible; it gains financial resources, establishes our schedules and our recreation. We meet a new person and the first thing we ask is "What do you do?" The reply sets their status in our mind. To be jobless and broke is a crisis on many levels.

After hearing Glazer's talk I stressed that my clients needed to work, no excuses. I did not force specific jobs on them, but I required that they have some kind of job. My personal desire was to find each client's real interests.

I am amazed at how we humans view problems. We worry we are too young or too old, too rich or too poor. We pick and choose the issues. Most of us handle about five worries at a time—if we solve a problem another pops up. We live with a never-ending supply of worries, which can cause depression.

Unknown people, places, and things can provoke fear. Fear can be eased by friendships. Sharing our thoughts forces us to organize them and sort out current concerns. We learn that sharing helps us balance our worries and because of this we learn to trust others.

People who deny that they have problems are dull or dishonest. Everyone has worries that induce emotions, even if we are not aware of the influence. Part of living a full life is learning to face worries and to take control of our reality.

It is true that coercion, whether direct or indirect, is a part of supervision, but it must be limited, not cruel, to be effective. I was not a real friend to my clients. My role was to ensure public safety, and that was what consumed my days.

* * *

If clients saw that my office was dark they returned to the first floor and the elevator operator, Ellen, reported their visit to me. She knew my clients and could tell if they were stressed. I was thankful for her help.

One missed encounter was a man wearing cowboy boots, his hat in hand. His companion, an attorney, was in a dark suit. They told Ellen they would return at 11 a.m. When I found out, I checked in with Carl Johnson, who told me the man had taken a plea in Tuttle's court. Normally I had thirty days to finish pre-sentence reports, but Tuttle wanted the hearing within the week, before summer break.

Carl said the defendant, Bill, was from an old-line family. His crime was fraud, by way of selling a herd of cattle four different times and supplying culls; baiting and switching was illegal in cattle sales. Bill had pled to grand larceny.

Carl's file showed Bill had a prior arrest in Oregon, where he had pled guilty. He received probation but had failed to pay restitution or court costs, so Oregon had issued a warrant. Bill was now offering to pay restitution with a loan taken out on part of his family's land.

At eleven, Bill's hat dropped on my desk, his attorney in tow. His attorney summed up the case and gave me a copy of the charging information. He asked about the scope of my report, as if he had not read prior pre-sentences.

"Our pre-sentences are like Oregon reports," I said. "The judge decides if you get a copy. Normally you do."

The suited attorney started interviewing me.

"Slow down," I said. "I will talk to the judge and see Bill tomorrow at 9 a.m."

The suit said he had to leave for Portland.

"Mail your remarks to Judge Tuttle," I told him. "Bill can expect a two-hour meeting. Tuttle wants a quick turnaround."

Hat in hand, Bill and the suit left unhappy. Tuttle would tell me where he stood on the case.

As the elevator shut, I headed to Carl's office to see if his secretary would type my report. My typing was normally done in Pasco or Spokane, but if Tuttle was going to get a quick report, Carl and his secretary would have to help.

At first glance the crime was a carbon copy of Bill's prior crime. In Oregon he had sold a herd three times to three separate buyers and bought cull cattle for delivery. He had paid no restitution and he had not learned his lesson.

Carl and Judge Tuttle expected restitution for victims. A trial would be long, complicated, and messy. If restitution was paid, the victims would get their money and the fall docket would be smaller. Tuttle knew Bill's history, so my report could be brief.

Bill visited me once more but his story had more holes than swiss cheese. I was concerned with restitution, but Bill just talked about his farm. "What is he trying to sell me?" I wondered. My interest was piqued so I visited the courthouse to check on his tax payments.

I found that Bill had shifted his assets—his farm and government land leases—to his son. Bill was legally broke; he was trying to pull a fast one. I attached the tax paperwork to my court report. I proposed that Bill go to prison, but he got probation; a deal was a deal.

Upset, I put Bill on weekly report until he started paying restitution. A week later Bill reported, appearing more humble. His son, now in control, had asked him to leave.

His son offered Bill a job as a sheepherder on leased land in Grand Round, Idaho, and in Oregon near Clarkston. The son wanted Bill gone, but I still wanted restitution. I agreed to Bill's job on the condition that all of Bill's wages were garnished to pay restitution.

Bill agreed. "He can wheel and deal to sheep," I thought. A prodigal father would labor in the wild as the victim. When I left town a year later he was still paying restitution every month.

* * *

It helps to be visual when making a point. Say it, show it, and repeat it was my theory. I came up with the idea to draw a circle on paper and cut it into eight sections. I asked clients to list their goals, and I accepted them or negotiated. I sought eight options on a continuum from easy to hard. I labeled each section of the paper circle with an option. We negotiated sanctions—a failure might mean two days in jail, a crime always meant prison.

Once a circle was completed, a client selected an option. I did not press for a particular choice. Each time the client failed, he received a sanction and picked a new option from the circle. If all selections were used, we started over.

We had a contract of sorts—clients selected their options, but I was in control. If questions arose, we brainstormed options to deal with specific habits or problems.

Larry was my first client to use the circle. He was in his mid-thirties. He drank and wrote bad checks. His drinking was legendary, and it had cost him his job, his marriage, and his freedom. Larry, however, was in denial, and he tested me. He showed up to a meeting drunk and got two days in jail.

Mad but sober, Larry looked at his options. He wanted out of jail, so he accepted my game. His first option had said, "I won't drink." Since he had failed that one, he chose another from the list: find a job, go to AA, find new friends, get inpatient treatment, or go to church. Any time he drank, it was two days in jail and he chose a new option. If he wrote a bad check, it was prison. We would repeat our scheme until he stopped drinking.

Eventually I was on his mind more than drinking. He said he would go to AA, but a week later he called me from a bar. I met him at jail.

Upon release, Larry selected "Inpatient at White Swan," which was a treatment program near Prosser, Washington.

He knew I would not back off. After three months at White Swan he was released. He worked and attended AA. He was in control, but still I was on his back.

Controlled choices seemed to work well with addicts. It allowed offenders options, yet held them accountable. I found it effective without having to use excessive threats.

If a client's choice was legal, I supported it. Consequences were less important than daily performance and positive results.

Observing people setting goals provided insights into their future conduct. I also took note of who ran with whom. Associates shared interests, values, and activities. Clients who hung out with shortsighted folk were more likely to commit another crime.

Rapport with my clients was necessary and when we trusted each other the results were better. Knowing a client's values was important, as it helped prevent misunderstandings.

For instance, to one client, the word friend could mean a person who helps and never hurts. To another it could mean a person sharing time, space, interests, or goals, whether positive or negative.

Of friends, Henry David Thoreau said, "My Friend shall forever be my Friend, and reflect a ray of God to me."

* * *

Theories that advocated profile tests implied that conduct was predictable. They sought certainty in statistical formulas. But tests and formulas cannot convert intangible qualities, such as feelings, into quantifiable data.

I had trouble with issues of free will, such as suicide. We can understand human choice only if we consider acts in the context of quality by considering emotions and feelings, which heighten or restrict one's capacity to perform.

Humans harm others in acts of lust, greed, power, and self-interest. Age and immaturity are sometimes factors. Mature adults have a capacity to act within borders in time and space, and in positive ways.

People with mental illness live a distorted reality that limits this capacity. Only with therapy or medication can they interact with the same reality that normal people see.

I learned these truths slowly; supervision was a kind of apprenticeship, an art built by practice, in which most learning curves lasted years.

I preferred to supervise probationers, as parolees had experienced prison life. Probationers felt lucky for the chance to avoid prison. Citizens get their best value in diversion efforts, not incarceration, as 80 percent of diverted criminals do not reoffend. The public avoids prison costs and offenders' lives are positively altered. Prisons are often crime colleges or hate factories, so parolees often leave prison with some degree of rage. Inmates carry the baggage of anger, and 40 percent reoffend.

* * *

There was a constant debate about the relative value of rehabilitation versus justice. Advocates for offenders saw offenders' rights as above public safety. My mentor, Dave Schafer, taught me that public safety was paramount. Yet Dave never said, "Three strikes and you do life in prison without parole."

In 1967 some field staff members who were averse to politics withheld their involvement in legislative matters. Regrettably, their inaction eroded public safety as legislation changed functions of field staff, police, courts, and the corrections system.

Powerful forces butted heads in Seattle and Olympia. I was isolated in rural Washington, so remote that my news arrived as history.

When field services was transferred to the Department of Institutions in July 1967, it meant that people whose focus was on prison issues would oversee probation supervision.

Legislators controlled sentences, but prison leadership tried to control releases. The parole board, concerned with public safety, wanted slower releases, but the prisons sought early releases to manage overcrowding.

Other reform laws were passed in 1967, including work release (WR), which was a major change in the field. Few citizens noticed the twenty-bed school release program at the University of Washington.

County and state work release units also opened, and state social workers' influence grew, supported by the Washington Council on Crime and Delinquency. The council pushed for the hiring of ex-felons in field offices. Lawmakers passed twenty-eight changes to the RCW 72 laws to make it possible, and soon ex-felons were hired in Tacoma and Seattle. The ex-felons' employment turned life upside down for the rest of our staff, as there were concerns about devaluing our mission of safety.

In Seattle and Tacoma, seven ex-offenders were hired by a lottery method. Most were fired within months. The effort was a step back, as police and courts withheld data from our offices for fear that felons would share it. There were crimes, bad behavior, and drug use among the ex-offenders.

The transition required a great effort to realign our operations with prisons. We learned institutional language and had to adapt to new ways of thinking.

A transfer from Tacoma, Pete, told me about the hiring of offenders there. He then asked if he could be hired also. "What the hell is going on?" was my first thought. It made no sense, but it was the law, and my job was not to write the law but to implement it.

Pete missed one detail—he needed my blessing and I did not give it. Pete had no job history and had been in and out of prison for twenty years; he was not trustworthy.

I told Pete, "Find a job and work for a year. Then we'll talk."

He knew I was serious and found work at a gas station that paid $3 per hour. It would help his case if he finished a GED. Pete met that challenge and enrolled at a community college.

Pete lost his job after harvest, but hired on at a gas station in Dayton. He hitchhiked to work. Months flew by, and eventually Pete arrived to collect on our deal. I prepared his paperwork.

Pete moved to Tacoma to enter the program. He earned a bachelor's degree, and after graduation he made probation and parole officer trainee status and worked twenty years for our agency. He was a hard-nosed officer on people who didn't work. Under Pete's supervision, it was work or jail.

* * *

The Hill was a place where power ruled. Inmates grouped themselves as blacks, Native Americans, Mexicans, lifers, and bikers, and each group sought power. The con bosses were the meanest, smartest, and toughest, and knew the most about other inmates in their cellblocks.

When I visited the Hill I saw glimpses of life in cellblocks and heard rumors in the breezeways. The prison guards were extensions of Warden Rhay and their word was final. Still, they gave con bosses a certain space, and that arrangement met everyone's needs.

One inmate from Spokane, Buddy, had a wife on probation. She lived in Walla Walla and worked at the Apple Café. Linda Chapman, her officer from the Spokane office, asked me to check on Bonnie to verify she and Buddy were moving to Spokane upon Buddy's release. They could not stay in town because Buddy was not from Walla Walla.

On Buddy's release date, Bonnie was to pick him up at 10 a.m., but asked to work extra at the café. She was worried that Buddy would make a scene, so she asked a guard to tell Buddy to relax, as she would arrive by noon. Buddy was not a patient man.

Bonnie arrived at noon to find that Buddy's release had been postponed until midnight because of illegal communications. The guard was fired for the rule violation.

* * *

I denied two heavy-duty parolee cases that I had inherited in 1966. The first had killed an unsuspecting drunk in a bar fight in Yakima. He hit his victim with a beer mug and the man died. The man absconded and I never saw him.

The second case was a parolee in Dayton who refused to report. I finally found him and said, "Report or I'll arrest you." It was the only time I saw him. He asked for a transfer to Pasco for work and when he was accepted I transferred his file.

Man struggles until he learns to live with his troubles. To grow up, a person must become aware of his personal flaws. It is not until we accept our weaknesses that we can learn to live well.

I wanted to know what caused my clients' worries. A key to knowing a person was to listen to their beliefs. Beliefs color a person's perception of the world. Faith links us to a higher being. All cultures have spiritual beliefs of some kind, even if not religious. There are mainstream religions, but also luck, ancestor worship, mother earth, and various other gods.

Society's code of conduct is based on Judeo-Christian beliefs and historic European laws. In corrections there is a process that parallels the religious idea of forgiveness and rebirth. It starts with "I'm sorry. I will do better." In both religion and corrections, we must admit our errors, ask forgiveness, and redirect our life after a failure.

Not surprisingly, remorse and guilt mix with faith and rebirth inside jails. Whether remorse is real or contrived, inmates have time to reflect while in our penitentiary system.

Corrections may be rooted in moral reform, but jail is not uplifting because it is the antithesis of a free society—people lose the ability to choose. Inmates are stripped of identity, friends, and possessions. Confinement compels obedience and imagination is the sole legal escape.

The first objective of inmates in jail is survival; the weak or distracted fade quickly. Inmates choose to be helpful or hurtful to each other. Some find distraction in abusing others.

While doing supervision I watched clients make daily choices. My ability to arrest without a warrant was crucial to gaining clients' attention. It made clients aware that probation was an extension of custody. It was freedom, but with a set of conditions.

It was not forgive and forget, it was "Here is a ladder to citizenship, now climb it."

* * *

Washington State's economy slowed in 1967 as the Department of Institutions reformed our agency as the Division of Probation and Parole. Boeing had a cyclical downturn, and the state focused on budget cuts. The Department of Institutions developed a prisoner classification process to help control costs. Classification was meant to sort troublemakers from lower-risk cases. Requirements for classifying someone as low-risk grew lenient, which cut costs because low-risk offenders got no supervision.

Probation eroded with this new thinking. We were forced to play a lottery, trying to figure out who would do well without supervision. Staffers selected cases based on agency criteria and demands for cutting costs, not based on court agreement or public safety.

Parole cases naturally failed more often than probationers, so probation became a dummy status as parole cases got all the supervision.

Enter Mr. Ramsey Clarke, an ex-United States Attorney General. In Seattle he gave a speech on why and how society was liable for crime. Criminals were not at fault, he said. Rather, society sets up black people and the poor for failure, so we must ensure civil rights. Clarke declared that staff members making arrests without a warrant was an abuse of power.

Clarke's view carried the day. Fred Finsley's thinking was now officially confirmed. While I appreciated Finsley's simplified formats, I had real concern about our agency's major shift to an institutional way of thinking.

* * *

We had good news at the Heffernan house in the spring of 1968. Kathy was nearing the delivery date of our first child. At St. Mary's Hospital we faced a long day. If Kathy took medication she would have fallen asleep.

Finally Kathy's doctor checked on her. I joined him as he changed into scrubs for her delivery. He smoked a big cigar as he dressed. He assured me that in years of doctoring he had not lost a father. Relax, he told me.

On May 28, 1968, Kathy gave birth to a boy, Shawn. It was dark out when I called family in Spokane with the news. "We had a healthy son," I said. "Kathy did fine."

* * *

No one noticed that I made so few arrests even as my caseload grew to 135 cases. Yet humble times awaited me in Clarkston, where a client named Joe hung around with teenagers. He and others had broken into a drugstore. Joe's young codefendants went to juvenile court; he went to superior court.

It was clear at our first meeting that Joe would not accept a second chance. His parents did not care; Joe was an only child who lived at home, did not work, and could do no wrong.

I sold freedom, but Joe was not buying. I knew I needed to get his attention, yet I was in town just one day per week. I told Joe he had to find work. He made no effort, so eventually I said, "Find a job or I will arrest you."

I knew Judge Jordan would not support me at a hearing, but at least Joe would see the inside of jail before a court appearance. I hoped that would get his parents' attention.

On my next trip to Clarkston I found Joe in jail. He had sold drugs from that first burglary. In my report I recommended prison. Judge Jordan was agreeable with children at risk. When I told Joe of my report a flash of grief crossed his face. He learned the hard way that it was not a game. He said he was sad and sorry.

The night before Joe's 9:30 a.m. hearing in Asotin, I stayed in Clarkston. I worked on reports until 2 a.m. and didn't wake up until 9:15. I called Asotin to say I would be late, shaved, dressed, and sped south.

Jordan was on the bench as I entered. Joe was at the attorney's table. His family was in the front row. When I was called forward I talked for just four minutes. I had now embarrassed Judge Jordan, and he was mad. Citizens would start to question how he ran his court.

Jordan ignored my report and Joe continued on probation. I had no appeal. Asotin's jail was in a basement and I stopped there after I apologized to the court. I took a deep breath.

Joe sat in the waiting room. He was not smiling. He knew that if I had been on time, he would now be on a bus to prison.

He was worried that I was out to get him, and I knew I had his attention. He decided to take his second chance seriously.

"Your slate is clean," I told him. "What's over is over. You need to follow the rules now. No special conditions have been added by the court, nor will I add any."

However, it was still strike one. Joe got a job, avoided old friends, and went to AA. I had not been aware of a drinking problem. Joe decided that his freedom was vital, so he was reborn a true believer. Me not waking up allowed him a chance to take a straight and narrow road.

* * *

Ken was a client of mine who was paroled after serving eighteen years for assault. I had met him while he was still at the WSP. Ken had mental issues, and while in prison he had evolved two personalities. Ken's file was thick, but there had been no mental history when he entered prison in the 1940s. There were no psychological reports in his files. Some prisoners feign mental illness to avoid conflicts with other inmates, and as a result Ken's illness had gone untreated.

One Ken appeared as an educated man studying ancient Indian tribes of Brazil. He had fabricated a history, a language, and an imaginary dictionary he kept in boxes in his cell. He was proud of his work.

Just as the professor was proud, Ken's second personality, a wild-eyed explorer, was afraid of his own shadow, fearful his work may be stolen. Explorer Ken's eyes darted as he saw danger all around him. I could not talk to Ken when the fear gripped him.

A tall, thin man in his fifties, Ken had deep-set eyes, unkempt hair, and a three-day beard. Ken's personalities were mood-driven, and he was easily confused. He had refused parole just to keep his books together. On parole, he found a place to live and a job at the cannery in Dayton.

Ken missed two report days, so I stopped at his hut in the Green Giant housing compound. He was not there. A clerk in the company office confirmed Ken still worked there. I was not worried that Ken would cause trouble, but he made people uncomfortable. I walked through the plant but did not find Ken.

I finally found Ken in his 12 x 8 ft. dirt floor cabin at 6 a.m. His only pieces of furniture were two wooden chairs, a table, and a cot. Two boxes in a corner held his work.

Ken did dirty work at the cannery. He needed clean clothes and a shower. He told me he liked his job, but was nervous. He had heard there would be layoffs in three weeks. That brought out the anxious explorer conquered by fear.

I saw panic and tears, stress and worry. I said if he needed me to I would keep his work in my trunk. Still, I realized he could not be homeless, so I offered to check for jobs. Ken was often confused and had a hard time meeting people, which made job-hunting difficult.

I remembered Bill, the wayward cattle salesman now herding sheep in the wild. I thought that job might work for Ken. He would live alone. He liked dogs. We agreed to meet on the courthouse steps in Dayton on Monday at noon.

Herders signed up for a year in the wilderness. The sheep owner supplied dogs, a wagon, food, and the sheep. I found one owner who would interview Ken. The owner said it was difficult to find people willing to live alone. I was not sure which Ken would show up on Monday, but when we met at noon he was in clean clothes with his hair combed.

The quiet professor had a nice, quiet interview and was hired. I gave Ken enough report forms to last a year, and his boss agreed to mail Ken's reports. The last I saw of Ken was his backside as he tossed his bags and boxes into a pickup truck. Ken had a home again.

I talked with Ken's boss every month. He told me Ken liked living in the wilderness, the sheep, and the dogs.

* * *

In 1968 I was asked to join the board of Catholic Charities. When I agreed my name began to surface for other community boards.

Chuck Austin, a WSP supervisor, asked me to attend a local alcohol information meeting. The meeting was the Washington State Health Department's effort to establish an alcohol and information referral center in Walla Walla. Twenty people attended, some with experience in writing bylaws.

We elected a president. Then, jokingly, Austin offered my name as vice president. I protested and turned it down, but when I was assured I would have no duties I accepted.

At the first meeting, the alcohol division director of health spoke and informed us that if we raised local funding, the health department would match it, dollar for dollar, up to fifty thousand dollars.

Our president had business contacts and felt he could raise the funds. We set a date to hear his report. It looked like things would be accomplished easily, and I felt great.

But soon the president was forced to resign after he was arrested for driving while intoxicated. Suddenly I was president of the Walla Walla County Council on Alcoholism.

I called a meeting to elect a new president; I did not want the job. When the former president's wife dropped off the bylaws, she told me she believed the pressure of fundraising had caused his stress and problems.

During the special meeting I had called, no one accepted the positions of either president or vice president. I was stuck. But at least the members would help me, and we set dates to visit the city council and the board of county commissars.

I spoke at both meetings and got moral support but no money. Chuck Austin moved to Pennsylvania; he would be no help in raising funds.

The health department offered to help our effort, but I had no fundraising background. I was a state worker and did not know if I could ask citizens for money. I learned that AA members did not raise funds for alcohol causes. The dollar per meeting for coffee was the limit. Private donors were my sole option.

By mid-February 1969 I had zero dollars. I was ready to resign in March, but before I did, I took a day off to canvass door to door. I figured if I saw no results I would resign.

I started on the east side of town and worked toward the center, even stopping at businesses. I planned to ask for money until it was dark or I reached downtown. It would be my best and last effort. If it was unsuccessful it would mean town folk were not ready for this project.

I had no results on the first nine stops. Then one business owner asked, "Who have you signed up?"

"No one," I answered.

I decided not to ask for money. Instead I asked, "How do I raise funds in this town?"

He said, "You're doing okay but you need one donor to start you out."

He pulled out his checkbook and wrote me a $1,000 gift. He had a brother who had died a drunk. "This gift is for him," he said.

I bounced out to my car and worked toward downtown. I gathered $30,000 in pledges and checks by 5 p.m.

I was ready for our next meeting. Members were inspired, and secured cash and in-kind gifts of an office, office equipment, and even furniture. By the end of March we had reached our fundraising goal.

Volunteers opened and staffed the information and referral office, and I resigned as president. The office continues to give information and treatment services. I learned not to join future boards without knowledge of the commitment they would require.

* * *

In spring 1969 I attended a talk by Secretary of State Lud Kramer at Pete's Broiler. Kramer talked broadly and abstractly about the Department of Social and Health Services for an hour. He asked for questions but the locals stayed quiet. To get discussion going, Prosecutor Art Eggers said that I, as a state employee, might have comments. I was put in a difficult spot.

I had never been briefed on the DSHS plans; I only saw how field staffers struggled within the Department of Institutions. I felt that my issues would be too specific for Kramer. Art baited me again by recalling a topic we had discussed at coffee. "What is your version of the correct method to introduce change?" he asked.

I said that agency consolidations tangled different cultures and missions, and some priorities were ignored. I knew of no DSHS plan to guide the consolidation; I saw smoke and mirrors.

"Can anyone clarify the DSHS governance scheme that will exist in two years?" I asked.

My question was brief and unfriendly. But Kramer was kind and did not attack me. He smiled and said nothing. His silence proved my point.

* * *

In June 1969 I transferred back to Spokane. Before I left Walla Walla I revisited the penitentiary, where Warden Bobby Rhay, with his strong personality and hard work, had kept order for twenty-one years.

To keep peace, Rhay used special paroles to local farmers who provided jobs to con bosses as a favor to Rhay. The jobs helped hardcore inmates submit parole plans for the parole board. A con boss leaving the Hill distracted the inmate population and created power struggles.

During my three years in town, depression had hung like a fog over the Hill. I had gone there for oral boards, pre-parole duty, and other sessions. My second oral board was memorable.

The oral panel was for the brother of one of Rhay's helpful farmers. The man was a candidate for a counselor job. He had no background in corrections, so I asked him why he wanted the job. I expected to hear it was because the pay was good or the work was steady.

He simply replied, "The Lord called me."

Alarm bells rang in my head.

"How does the Lord speak to you?" I asked.

"God always speaks last. The devil argues first."

I gave him a score of zero. I did not sit on another oral panel.

* * *

Supervisor Linda Chapman, two field staffers, and a secretary took my place in Walla Walla. Linda was hired to oversee the Pasco and Walla Walla offices. She was the first female probation and parole supervisor in the state. Before I left for Spokane I oversaw the painting and cleaning of a new office suite in the Jones Building.

Director of the Department of Institutions Dr. William Conte walked into my office just weeks before I left.

He was in a short-sleeve shirt, his tie loose. He was a tall man with a big smile who played with his glasses as he talked. Conte talked of historic Walla Walla, then shifted to the Hill. He was in town to meet Bobby Rhay for lunch and wanted me to join them. His hope was to reduce crime and limit prison growth, and he thought my input would be helpful.

"You know the community," he said. "You know the locals' views." His car was out front and ready to go.

Rhay greeted us on the front steps, wearing a tweed jacket with a dark tie. We had a brief tour through the shining hallways. The fields were green and well cared for. Life was quiet on the Hill. Our lunch was at the minimum-security section, a bit south of the main prison.

At lunch Rhay was gracious; he said nice things and acted like we were best friends. "Who is he talking about?" I wondered. Bob said I had a great work ethic, etc. It was a long lunch, and Rhay seemed to be playing poker.

As Conte drove me back to my office, he asked me how I saw Rhay.

What was I supposed to say? The man did not run a Sunday school. The truth was I saw the Hill as an emotional entity. I did not see operations; I sensed fear and felt anger in it.

The penitentiary was Conte's flagship in corrections. I was not aware that shortly he would send that ship into very heavy seas via a self-governance program called the resident government council (RGC). He sought to avoid the forces that had caused riots at Attica in New York.

Conte sent Rhay to Europe for three months to study Swedish, German, and French prisons. With Rhay gone, Conte tossed out rules. The superintendent did not regain control of the WSP until 1981.

* * *

Portland had a greater influence in Walla Walla than either Spokane or Seattle. The Snake and Columbia rivers were the gateway to the Pacific, but ideas and culture flowed upriver, not down from Spokane. Salesmen traveled from Seattle and Spokane, yet people read Portland's paper for barge or train schedules, as that's where products were headed.

During my time in Walla Walla I saw few transfers from Spokane and I did not see much heroin use. In fact my first heroin dependency transfer occurred just as I left. It was a young woman named Tammy who had schooled in Vancouver, British Columbia.

Her family was wealthy and she was smart and attractive, yet she was caught in a destructive habit. Tammy's eyes were vacant, and I found it unnerving. I investigated her transfer for Chapman.

Tammy's parents confirmed she had a place to live. They had contacted a Portland drug clinic. The cost was $3,000 per month. If she had a setback, Tammy, under a doctor's care, would go into treatment. Her parents would pay the costs. I finished her report and was ready to move.

I left Walla Walla as more than a one-man outpost. I admitted my surprise when Sheriff Klundt and his wife had Kathy and I over for a picnic. Art hosted staff, city police, and court officials.

My Walla Walla days helped define and clarify my career in corrections. Yet I did not see the big changes coming. The formation of the Department of Social and Health Services would bring on confusion, changes, and frustration.

Back in Spokane
1969–1971

During my time in Walla Walla, the Spokane office had moved four blocks, from the courthouse to the corner of Ash and Broadway. Our office building also housed the state personnel office. The move meant there was less of a bond with courthouse staff, and old contacts vanished in time.

East Sprague Avenue was the site of the new valley office. Bob Banta and Jerry Savland covered the valley and Adams and Whitman counties. Jim Northrup worked in Colville and supervised Stevens and Pend Oreille counties. Jim still did National Guard duty during the summer months.

Much had changed; there were new faces and new energy in the office. But Spokane was home, and I would not leave again.

Mom, Dad, and Patty still lived on Ermina Street. Kathy's folks lived on Napa Street. Both sets of grandparents were excited to watch their grandchildren grow, and we expected our second child in August. We lived with Kathy's folks to save for a down payment on a house.

In June we found a home in northwest Spokane and moved in furniture before closing. But delay after delay meant it was August 29 before we moved in; a day later, our second son was born. We named him Kelly.

Mom's health had turned poor—her heart was in bad shape, and she was no better after a visit to the hospital. Her heart condition limited her work and social life. Patty was working at Seafirst Bank, so Mom was home alone.

Mary and her husband Fred lived next door to my parents, which helped. Mom was not one to complain, but I saw the dark circles under her eyes. She took oxygen on her bad days. After Kelly was born she held him proudly and seemed better that summer. But in the fall and winter her health declined. There was nothing the doctors could do.

On January 11, 1970, an ambulance rushed Mom to Sacred Heart Hospital with major heart failure. We visited her that afternoon. She looked pale, but we did not expect her to die.

Mom's death was a shock. The cold winter winds stayed a bit later into the spring. Dad and Patty worked, and during the day the Ermina home sat silent.

* * *

The DSHS concept had been born after Evans met the black rioters in Seattle in 1964. Black youth felt abandoned by the lack of social resources but saw white people living well.

Lyndon Johnson's Great Society programs were not user-friendly, so President Nixon's scheme was less complex as he fine-tuned policies to create regionally responsive agencies. Nixon intended to starve federal agencies and shift power to regions. Governor Evans expanded upon the concept and in 1968 his task force recommended consolidating services into one agency.

In 1970, in an extraordinary legislative session, Senate Bill 52 consolidated five agencies with various missions into a super agency called the Department of Social and Health Services. Overnight, historic, disparate agencies were reorganized and now reported to new DSHS Secretary Sidney Smith.

Attempts were made to bundle services: welfare, healthcare, in- and out-patient mental healthcare, corrections, veterans' care, and childcare. The DSHS tried to stuff fifty pounds of duties into a ten-pound bag, but consolidation confused new providers and caused shaky, disorganized services.

DSHS leadership tried to communicate, coordinate, and standardize to cut costs. The helpful welfare culture collided with public safety with each having different questions and views based on their histories. Stakeholders hoped problems would vanish, but new ones emerged. Sidney Smith had set his priorities, but what worked on paper did not work in the real world. RCWs (laws) and Washington Administrative Codes (policy codes) did not fit. We needed new legislation, but bureaucrats dragged their feet, so laws were stretched and distorted by verbal directives. Small problems became a mess within the new super agency.

The DSHS utilized citizen input via regional committees. Each of the ten regions set standards and coordinated services, yet financial decisions were made in Olympia. The formation of the DSHS seemed to shift power, but it maintained the status quo behind a façade of grass roots symbolism.

DSHS planning and training were weak and bore bitter fruit.

Dr. Conte retired just as the DSHS and prison reform got underway.

* * *

I assumed Linda Chapman's Spokane caseload. It was the major trade-off in my transfer to Spokane. I had carried female cases in Walla Walla and Okanogan, and I had helped when Linda asked, but now I had eighty-five female clients. It was a big difference. Every day I was challenged with cultural issues.

Yet I remembered to start where clients were, and that made life easier. I added a box of Kleenex to my desk to deal with my female clients' best defense. After they cried, we got on with the issues at hand.

Good organization began with planning all my appointments. The receptionist at first disliked scheduling, but it paid off—our waiting room no longer had yelling kids, I saw my clients on time, and I was able to do my other work. I even had time for report writing.

I limited coffee sessions but gossip was part of the daily routine. We heard rumors of even more new changes. Bob Lizee, the regional administrator, and John Prideaux dealt with the DSHS daily.

The Department of Institutions move had changed the logo on our front door; now we became part of DSHS culture, which meant manuals of dos and don'ts to standardize our actions and the classification process. I disliked classification, as I doubted I could predict an offender's future conduct. There were many variables I could not control: work, family, friends, etc. A client had to live his or her own life.

The DSHS consolidation affected us beyond distraction. I tried to focus on my caseload and sell women the idea that their freedom was valuable. My method was low key; I let each client set goals and did not impose my own agenda.

Each woman needed an income, friends, goals, beliefs, and a method of dealing with her problems. I adjusted to the feminine reality that raising kids was work.

I talked with my clients about keeping house, kids, laundry, and being a good mother. Watching Kathy at home helped me understand what it meant.

I knew women expressed emotions differently, but I did not know why. I simply accepted the reality. Ladies could cry with dignity, as crying was a valid emotional release, yet their tears had little impact on me. I saw many crying styles, yet I did not reach over to comfort them. When a client cried, I waited it out and we moved on. I did not rescue cases. I helped them plan.

One of the biggest differences I noticed with my female caseload was that women tended to accept dependency while men resisted it.

Ten percent of the time, women lived in a relationship with partners who were unwilling to comply with supervision. Compliance was essential, but I felt I had no right to tell people how to live with others. I supplied options and hoped clients would find good outcomes with their partners.

Three halfway houses opened as safe living spaces in Spokane: Regina Hall, St. Margaret Hall, and Anna Ogden Hall. They were a gift for women in need. The facilities covered basic needs and helped with job searches and education.

Halfway houses did heavy work for those in trouble, yet I was hesitant to rely on them because I did not want to put a strain on their services. However, if a woman worked seriously, I called the houses for a placement.

* * *

Donna was in her mid-thirties and had once been pretty. She was no longer a beauty, though—a prostitute since the age of fourteen, she had been beaten too often by her pimp. Her street name was Shovel Face. Her face was a book of troubles and I wondered how she made a living on the streets.

I met Donna in jail after court. She was given probation for writing bad checks. She looked hopeless as she sat across the table from me, her head down.

I introduced myself and asked her what her plan was. "The street is out," I told her. "You are on probation for three years. You'll have to live legally or go to prison. How do you plan to do that?"

She glanced up but just looked lost. She avoided my question and waited for me to tell her what to do.

I repeated my question. "What's your plan?"

We sat there in the jail, both of us waiting.

"I can visit you again after you've had time to think. Is this afternoon better?"

Finally, Donna asked, "When do I get out?"

"I have no idea," I said. "I haven't heard a plan. You won't get out until you have a plan."

A flash of emotion crossed her face. Suddenly she was crying, the tears flowing. Her hand covered mine—it seemed like she was trying to comfort me. I already felt okay.

"When do you want me to come back?" I asked. "Today, tomorrow? I need a plan. With a plan you can get out."

Her hand pulled back and she glared at me.

"This is not a game," I said. "You will not get out without a plan. I can't make up a plan for you. I have no time to baby-sit you. I haven't lived on the streets and you wouldn't take my advice if I gave it. How will you stay out of jail?" I waited for her response, but she was quiet. "I'll see you tomorrow, or I'll see you Monday." I stood up.

"This afternoon," she replied.

It took a clever person to live on the streets. Without prostitution I was simply removing one of her sources of money. She had other options.

Sure enough, that afternoon, Donna had a plan. I turned down pieces of it as we negotiated. She had to replace her circle of weird friends and her wild habits.

She would move to a rooming house and get a job. She told me that Andy, a boyfriend, was a positive part of her life.

I met Andy over coffee. He had done jail time twice so he knew a judge's power. He was not bright, but he cared for Donna. He worked junking scrap metal. He was shorter than Donna but wide and strong as a bull. He understood that her lifestyle would have to change.

"I'll help and we will work through it together," Andy said.

Donna found work at a bakery and both she and Andy attended AA. In the past, Andy had liked drinking and Donna would drink if he drank. They found new friends. Months later I approved their marriage. When Alice Herdener was hired I turned Donna's file over to her. I saw Donna only to say hello.

I was able to have a male caseload again. I told my ladies to be good, and life returned to normal.

Two years passed, and then I got a call from Donna. She was in Sacred Heart Hospital. She asked me to visit, and when I walked into her room I found her very sick. Her skin was ashen and her voice raspy. Andy was sitting at her side.

She thanked me for coming. The cancer tests were not good; she had days to live.

"Do you remember our first meeting?" Donna asked.

"Yes, in the jail," I said.

"Thanks for that visit. Andy and I had three great years. We would not have had them if you had not made me choose."

Working with women like Donna taught me how to give a client space and control.

* * *

After handing over my female cases to Herdener there was a shuffling of clients to build my caseload. In that shuffle I gained Alex, a California parolee with a drug history.

Alex was strange. His file showed he had asked to serve his full term. He had refused the good time credit he'd earned and did ten years flat.

Alex had also had a prior arrest and probation. His ten years in prison were for his second arrest in California. He ran marijuana from Mexico to San Francisco. He tried to outrun the state patrol and crashed, killing his wife and daughter.

Alex was Mexican American and had been raised in Los Angeles. His passion was cars with high-powered engines, and he raced stock cars. He had started running marijuana in high school to make money for car parts. He had made fifty runs from Mexico without a hitch.

He married his high school sweetheart. Their first child was a girl and he tried to be a good husband and dad.

On a routine traffic stop, an officer saw a bag of marijuana on his front seat. He received probation but kept driving. He had no way to make a living, so he used marijuana to steady his nerves.

Alex knew a second arrest would mean jail time, but he risked prison even though he had some money in the bank. On his last run from Mexico, against his own rules, his wife and daughter joined him as his cover. Then flashing lights pulled in behind him.

His supercharged Buick hit 120 miles per hour. The trooper ate his dust. Alex looked for an exit, knowing the police would call ahead and he could not outrun a radio.

Just as he took an exit, a car darted into his lane. Alex overreacted and his car went airborne. He heard screams.

He woke days later chained to a bed. He was told his wife and daughter had died in the crash.

In prison, friends from his gang approached him. He told them he would not rejoin them, but they still wanted him back. He moved to Spokane to get away from his past, and that was how he became my case.

I was shocked at Alex's openness as he told his story. He had money in a California bank but had no interest in it. A broken man, he worked in a motorcycle shop and wanted to live a life to respect his wife and daughter.

"Tell me what to do," he said, "and I'll do it."

Weeks later Alex arrived at my office with his employer. He wanted his boss to know his past. His boss told me that Frank was a good mechanic who brought in work.

Months passed, then Alex came in upset.

Old gang pals had contacted his parents in Los Angeles. He shared an account in Los Angeles that held $450,000. The gang wanted him as a contact for drug shipments into Washington.

The account tied him to the gang. Alex felt they had violated his family. He said he had warned them to leave his parents alone but he knew the pressure would not stop.

"What can I do?" he asked.

I told Alex about a Drug Enforcement Agency task force.

"Alex, there are risks," I said. "Informers risk death."

But Alex was unconcerned. He had promised his family he would live right and he would die to uphold that.

"Set up a meeting," he said.

I reminded Alex that his parole status would not change if he met with the task force. He would still have to follow parole conditions.

Alex met with the federal agents, who moved him to Colville, where Jim Northrup assumed his supervision.

I heard nothing for a year. Then I had coffee with a friend in the federal courthouse, and a DEA agent at the table told me about Alex.

Alex had helped them crush a national drug network ranging from Kansas City to Cincinnati, Denver, and California. He had refused money and witness protection after testifying.

Historically, Mexican American children worked the fields, but Alex's parents had worked when he was growing up, so he had joined a gang to survive. Gang members filled a vacuum in high school as both his parents worked.

Childhood events shape how people deal with love, hate, anger, and courage. Broken upbringing can cause ruinous adult behavior. Emotional stability is as important as intelligence. To know love is to feel the glue that makes up human relationships.

Love is never an earned quality. It is a gift from a person with the capacity to love. The more someone loves, the more he or she is able to love. Yet, as with all emotions, it is a use-it-or-lose-it deal.

* * *

In 1970, a face from my past appeared in an aisle at a Safeway store. It was the county jailer who had lived above the Walla Walla jail. He was retired, and said that Elize was still doing time in prison.

He asked me if I would talk to Spokane's Salvation Army center on Elize's behalf. I agreed, and soon saw a pre-parole request from Elize to the Salvation Army center. Their staff agreed to help find Elize a job, so he was paroled to Spokane. He looked younger now that he had dried out. Within a week he reported that he had found work with a Salvation Army forestry crew near Forks, Washington.

After confirming the job I accepted his travel request and shipped his file to Port Orchard, Washington. A month later I got news that Elize had died; a death certificate followed. Elize had fallen off a cliff in the woods. I wrote my summary to the parole board, and with the death certificate attached I closed my file to Olympia.

* * *

I was in the office around noon on a Friday in May 1970 when Detectives Gene and Jerry McGougan rushed in. There was a rumor that the ski mask bandits were in a Browne's Addition apartment and they needed an officer to join their raid.

The ski mask bandits, parolees Bobbie and Cecil, wore ski masks to rob remote taverns. They had robbed six taverns, and police felt it was only a matter of time with drunks and guns before someone would be shot.

Both parolees had active parole warrants and a history of armed robberies. Bobbie was allegedly in town to place flowers on his mother's grave for Mother's Day the following Sunday.

"Will you come?" the detectives asked me.

I agreed.

The tip said both men were in a second-floor apartment. Jerry checked to verify the number and got a key. We approached the apartment and found the door open and quiet. The brothers looked at each other and we rushed in with guns ready.

I went first and dropped down. The detectives passed me and secured the apartment. It was eerie. A television was on in the front room, a pot of water boiled on the stove. Pictures and keys were on a countertop, yet the apartment was vacant.

Jerry called for an area search. The keys on the counter fit a blue Cadillac in the parking lot; the car's trunk was loaded with guns and ammo. We had hit a jackpot but found no bandits.

Normally, if guns were involved, policy required a sergeant and four officers to perform an arrest—two at the front door, two in back. But the ski mask raid was based on a hot tip. Gene thought the pair had seen Jerry at the manager's office and fled. We were lucky they ran and did not fight.

I later heard that both suspects were killed in a shootout with police near Bakersfield, California.

* * *

Aaron was a young man who had broken into a house near his west-side home. At our first meeting I saw that Aaron was mentally limited. His school records confirmed my assessment. I did not expect much but I told myself to start where Aaron was.

I asked, "What do you want to do down the road?"

Aaron looked up and said, without blinking, "I'd like to be a brain surgeon."

I was in trouble. I couldn't just tell Aaron he lacked the brainpower to be a doctor.

"We'll work on it," I said. "To be a doctor, you must finish high school. Doctors need an education. First things first."

He agreed to return to an alternative high school.

Aaron had an uphill battle. I called Phil, the human resource director at Sacred Heart Hospital. Years before, Phil had worked in juvenile corrections at Mission Creek Honor Camp.

I asked, "Do hospitals have work for people with an IQ in the high eighties?"

Phil said he knew doctors he suspected had even lower IQs. But seriously, he said, there were jobs doing laundry. He said there was always turnover. I talked to Aaron and told him that if he went to school for two months with no missed classes, I would refer him to Sacred Heart's laundry facilities.

Months passed with good reports. I sent Aaron to see Phil, who hired him. Aaron saw the bloody sheets from surgery and lost interest in being a doctor. He decided he preferred laundry work. After Aaron received his GED he went on to community college.

Aaron met a young woman there and they talked about marriage after he finished probation. Years later I saw Aaron on the streets. He still worked in the laundry, had gotten married, and was doing well.

Aaron's story made it clear that good planning required that I help clients find their future, whatever it might be, as long as it was legal.

It would have been wrong for me to tell Aaron he had limits and could not dream of a better life. I learned that positive help was often the correct medicine. Aaron's story later became one of my interview questions for prospective employees: "What do you do if a client with a low IQ wants to be a doctor?"

* * *

Starting in June 1972 I experienced some career change as I became more involved in systems and operational processes and less involved in casework. My work became task driven and political as I pressed for changes.

Sheriff William Reilly had started a work release program in Spokane after passage of RCW 161 in mid-1968, while I was still in Walla Walla. Sergeant Ray Stavig was named director of nonsupport cases. In 1969 Ray visited our Broadway office for coffee and referrals.

With Ray's visits, he and I became friends. I became interested in WR as a tool to gain clients' attention. WR gave us a way to get clients to invest in and show commitment toward gaining their freedom.

WR forced clients to walk the walk. It had limited risks and kept clients focused on living legally. I felt it was a great tool. I saw positive results with limited public risk.

* * *

As I focused my energy on work release, the super agency rollout was ongoing. The DSHS had been poorly conceived and was poorly carried out. Managers found wiggle room in policies and there were no internal audits. Directives were ignored or forgotten, but there was no paper trail.

Managers were given abstract guidelines and metaphors, but decisions were not placed in context. State auditors' hair turned gray as verbal guidelines replaced written policies.

The DSHS secretary had final authority; old agencies existed in name only as Evans's concept of organization decentralized functions to regions. Leadership was ignoring what had worked well for me: start with people where they are, not where you want them to be.

In early 1971 the DSHS installed regional supervision of Spokane's probation and parole office and Bob Lizee moved to an office on Mission Street. His role was changed from eastern Washington administrator to region boss. He had managed all of eastern Washington but now had charge of only seven counties. The Yakima, Wenatchee, and Pasco offices floated off into other regions. The DSHS strategy had gaps, and planning was haphazard. Lizee fought to keep probation and parole operations as a single unit.

Bob butted heads with DSHS managers over dragging his feet on changes. He saw institutionalized confusion and resisted it. In addition, computer technology systems had just arrived, complicating the transition.

To computerize records, staff had to complete forms for the computers at Washington State University that were connected to Olympia. I had worked with computers at Old National Bank and I knew a range of applications, but the program the DSHS used was designed for research. Completed forms were stacked in storage, as the DSHS had yet to resolve how to enter data into the WSU mainframe.

We were also asked to do time and motion studies to collect quantifiable data on staff activity. Eighty percent of our cases were probationers, so most of our work related to the courts. Parolees and out of state supervision were the remainder.

* * *

In late summer 1971, parolees arrived from the WSP with reports from older, normally silent convicts. They said the penitentiary was a zoo, completely unsafe, with assaults, rapes, and drugs. Con bosses were running wild. The WSP staff stood aside, unable to control cellblocks.

I doubted the reports, but they kept coming and soon it was clear parolees had little to gain by lying, so I made inquiries; if half the stories were true, it meant the Hill had gone crazy.

Reports of violence and killings persisted. I was furious with department management for not stopping the crime and fear at the penitentiary.

I shared what I heard with Bob Banta, who had concerns and letters from families about violence running wild. It did not sound like the kind of Hill that Bobby Rhay would run.

One story had con bosses meeting chain buses to pick out "girlfriends" from the young arriving inmates. I called staff members I knew but got no clear answers, just weak denials.

Bob Banta and I went to Lizee and Prideaux with questions. They said they would check on the reports. The whole mess had a big brother feel to it. We wanted the public to know, but because we valued our jobs we stayed within our chain of command.

Weeks passed with no reply. We felt regional changes had affected communications, preventing local reports from going beyond the regional DSHS office. We followed up by contacting Prosecutor Don Brockett. Don said he would put a public voice to the reports but he needed statements—our information was only hearsay.

We were out on a limb so we took Don's advice and submitted a formal report to Olympia through Lizee and Prideaux. Brockett needed time to get statements from inmates. We allowed ninety days for Olympia to reply. Three months passed and we heard nothing.

On November 18, 1971, the *Spokane Daily Chronicle* headline read, "Brockett Raps Prisons on Drugs."

All hell broke lose as the story gained legs. Inmates had talked. Don was satisfied their stories were true. He did not mention Bob or myself. The Hill was a very hot potato.

Governor Evans said it was a political effort, and that Don wanted to make a name for himself as a candidate for governor.

The storm grew in the headlines, and Banta and I expected termination letters. Yet nothing came in the mail.

With a spotlight on the penitentiary day after day, Bob and I kept quiet but knew things would change. There were daily incidents: Brockett debated Evans, a furloughed inmate killed a state trooper, and an inmate called Saint Peter took part in the Take a Lifer to Dinner program and killed a druggist in Tacoma.

The public learned about many things: Blood Alley, a covered walkway at the WSP which was a killing location; *Concrete Mama*, a book written by an inmate with pictures of the Hill; "Jesse James," a lifer who escaped during the Take a Lifer to Dinner program. Putting the con bosses back in the bottle proved much more difficult than uncorking them.

* * *

DSHS managers during consolidation wanted stakeholders to rebuild networks. But local turf wars started even as the ink dried on consolidation; greed and pride lived. Ten regions were soon downsized to six.

I was assigned to a universal intake committee whose job was to create a common intake which would match agency services with applicants. The committee wrote a 180-page report which, counting the time invested, cost $125,000. The plan was that a general service center could do intake for welfare, corrections, veterans, and health services. The plan ignored whether services were voluntary or mandatory, one-time or long-term.

I disagreed with the approach and wrote, "Why treat welfare mothers as felons or felons as welfare mothers?"

The universal intake scheme died.

* * *

The city/county public safety building was set to open in 1970 and Ray Stavig asked for my help on a work release grant. Ray was asking the Law Enforcement Assistance Administration for funds to improve jail conditions.

I knew little about custody, so I had to learn about inmates and jails. State prisons had problems so I was not a welcome visitor there.

Rob Williams, who ran a sex offender unit at Western State Hospital, said he would approve my visit if I would commit to six visits over six months, and if Prideaux joined me. Rob wanted to educate outsiders about his unit. John Prideaux entered the north group and I the south group, each with twenty members.

Prior to entering the unit, candidates lived on ward for six months. Current members voted candidates into the groups. Members lived in open bays on wards for three years, and then did a year of ward release and a year of outpatient where they still lived on the ward but left daily to work a job in the community.

My ward was built circa 1940, with high ceilings and wide halls. It was quiet and clean. Members were involved in all phases of therapy planning and leadership. They provided security and set the scope of their therapy sessions, which were heavy duty: eighteen hours per day, six days a week of aversion brainwashing.

The program built egos, destroyed them, and then rebuilt them to alter thinking and habits. Therapy required total involvement—members were a leader one day, a target the next. I saw ward life as not useful to jails, what with high turnover mixed with con codes in the jail environment.

On January 20, 1971, we received certificates of completion as thanks for observing. Captain Byron Franz, the Spokane jail chief, endorsed our proposed program after he lived in a group in September 1970. Judges Willard Roe and George Shields also visited to assess the program.

In Spokane we created a simpler program: inmates in jail cellblocks first applied for the program. The next step was inside trustee, then outside trustee, and finally work release. Inmates justified their transfers by having no infractions. An infraction meant an inmate had to start over in the cellblock and reapply for the program. The idea was that an inmate's behavior would control his progress. To help inmates stay engaged, citizen volunteers visited three nights per week to ensure input and order.

Many things happened at work, but the home front was also busy. On October 4, 1971, Kathy had our third child, Michele. I was working days and also volunteering in the jail at night while Kathy was at home with three babies. I was not home much, so Kathy got help from her mother, Helen, and Auntie Rose.

* * *

We stressed that inmates could improve conditions by their conduct. Bob Enright, Chuck Lorraine, nine citizens, and I entered the jail. Chuck was an ex-offender. Bob was a staff volunteer.

We supported jail staff and inmates who followed the rules. In time, inmates were able to self-screen as volunteers brought fresh eyes. Offenders learned it was okay to help others, and soon they invested in the program and followed the rules.

I focused on my caseload and the new jail program. It was clear that being in custody caused depression and anger for offenders. Their stress was moderate to overwhelming, and inmates who were bored did harder time. It was easy for a negative culture and attitude to develop in cellblocks.

Untreated depression immobilized inmates, and thoughts of suicide were common. Volunteers brought a little of the outside into the jail, and knowing the outside world existed lowered inmates' stress and improved conduct.

Captain Franz opening his jail to citizens was a leap of faith, and I suspected that few others would have been so trusting. Betty

Winkler supplied our first volunteers by loaning us citizens from her pool of community volunteers. Betty's husband, Bob, was one of our first volunteers.

Once the program began, word of mouth spread as people talked about their experiences. Ultimately we had forty volunteers who, with no real authority, monitored and improved jail conditions. Inmates grew to trust volunteers, as their conversations were confidential except for what might impact jail safety. Jailers' jobs became less stressful, and they began to welcome volunteers.

Every week we brought outside values and positive energy into the cells. We met with volunteers before and after cell sessions to preview or debrief cell meetings, but volunteers got no special training—folks learned by doing. Half were women, some were couples or college students. All were at least twenty-one and had passed our record check.

Volunteers increased communication between staff and inmates. One woman came to group in a miniskirt. It caused a stir, but her presence boosted sign-ups for groups. She volunteered for two more years.

Five ex-POWs stationed at Deep Creek Survival School volunteered, led by Jim Shively. Jail inmates did not know the POWs' history and the men did not tell war stories. Jim, who had spent six years at the Hanoi Hilton, sat quietly and assured twenty-year-olds that, if they tried, they could survive a thirty-day sentence.

Sheriff Reilly would have preferred to transfer the jail to another agency. He saw it as a poor use of deputies; he wanted deputies to be on the road. He also feared jail costs might consume his budget, so he took Law Enforcement Assistance Administration money only to finish jail construction.

* * *

Sheriff Reilly wanted a court liaison for the jail to avoid any confusion and asked me to contact the superior court. I met with Judge Foley, who assigned Judge George Shields as court liaison.

Judge Shields took over in a heartbeat and asked District Court Judge Ben McInturff to join in. Together, Reilly, Shields, and McInturff developed the Spokane County Citizen Advisory Board made up of county commissioners, the Spokane County prosecutor, and four citizens appointed by county commissioners.

This group submitted a Law Enforcement Assistance Administration grant by Judge McInturff. The funds they received created a county corrections department and a probation unit for the district court. The money also funded reviews of Spokane County's justice system to provide input to commissioners.

In 1972, Jim Flynn was hired as county corrections director after Ray Stavig helped create a Washington State work release unit in the jail.

Bob Enright and I stayed busy with our caseloads and volunteered in the jail. I was lucky that Enright was blue-collar and skilled in dealing with jail staff. Whenever I got into hot water, he bailed me out.

We watched relations worsen between our staff and regional DSHS staff. Bernie Nelson, the DSHS regional administrator, consumed Lizee and Prideaux, who attended meetings and returned upset. The DSHS was putting no focus on corrections. I had first met Nelson in Wenatchee. He was intense. Hard feelings grew and conflicts got personal.

I watched field morale drop as the DSHS set policies and cut staffing levels and budgets for the field. Control over our budget meant control over our operations; we saw no relief. In time a rogue faction grew. Nelson supported work release, but his foot was on the neck of field staff.

Work Release
1971–1979

Jerry Savland, the first work release supervisor, had health issues and transferred to minimum service. I replaced Jerry in May 1972, just as the Spokane pot boiled. At first I reported to Bob Lizee, but soon I reported directly to Olympia.

My main interest in accepting the job was seeing jail self-screening put into practice. From a prison viewpoint, WR acted as a relief valve for overcrowding. There were other benefits, of course, but gaining bed space was a primary concern. Personally I saw little value in the use of WR as a re-entry tool unless it was part of an earn continuum in which good behavior and choices were rewarded.

With my promotion I received a raise and no longer carried a caseload. My staff was Jim Mott, Al Solinsky, and Greg Hare. My first months being the supervisor were a challenge. I had not planned on the promotion and I was not sure of my role. My boss was in Olympia, so I showed up daily but without a plan. Life was just different. Supervising staff was not the same as supervising probation and parole clients.

I did not like being the boss, but I had a certain status after working for years in the jail. I felt I could learn my role by managing WR cases. I made that decision before I talked to staff members, and my choice to carry cases put pressure on my staff. By doing it I had set policy, which was not my intent. My creativity with the cases also confused my staffers.

One upset staff member told me, "You're a lousy boss, but a great officer. Which do you want to be?"

His frankness hit me like a bucket of cold water. I was humbled and vowed to do better.

I realized I was not a co-worker; my staff wanted leadership, not extra hands. Staff would do the casework. My job was to create programs and to develop resources. I wanted to create a better work climate by sharing my vision and energy.

My actions confused the staff and they did not like my leadership style, so I was not shocked when all three staff moved to field jobs. Their move was a gift, but I did not see that immediately.

I started over with no baggage. I needed time to practice and think. When I worked as a probation officer clients distanced themselves because I confirmed their status as felons. In WR and prisons inmates gravitated to staff because staff controlled inmates' freedoms. I wondered what motivated inmates and how they would react to rules. And what did I believe?

I knew that WR cost a hundred times more per day than field supervision because of all the operational costs, so we needed to provide some value that justified the cost. The best justification was that higher-risk clients vetted their compliance and earned diversion. This meant the public avoided prison costs, as cases had jobs, incomes, or were involved in treatment programs.

Dick Issacson suffered as my first hire after my staff members left for fieldwork. I assigned him sixty cases, formerly managed by three different staff members. Dick worked hard for two months before I hired Tim Foley, then each of them carried thirty cases. I later hired Darlene Compton and each staff member carried twenty cases.

I needed committed staff, but we all had limitations and lives beyond work. It was important that I respect staff and not burn them out.

We benefited when staff worked together, communicating and sharing common goals. We cleared the air weekly and tried to enjoy each other. Conflicts get resolved and no one felt left out. I tried to anticipate staff members' needs and be proactive.

I set goals to improve communication with county staff. County custody worked 24/7, so they had the greatest influence on offenders. I mentored county staff to smooth out bumps and pushed for informal teamwork at the line level. County staff was the left hand and we were the right hand.

Weekly staff meetings raised interoffice awareness, opening dialogue and limiting mix-ups. We reviewed jobs, plans, fees, restitution, and home visits and updated each other on how we were doing. We set our priorities together, and when priorities were clear the work had context.

We had a division of duties but a common goal. Our objective was employment for every case, so we committed one day each week to job searches. It sent the message that we went beyond talking—we helped clients actually find work.

Our fourth child was born June 22, 1973, and named Timothy. Kathy had four children at home, all five years old or younger. If I had not had Kathy's support, I could not have been involved in the program.

* * *

Roy Lakewold, the chair of the WCA convention in Spokane, resigned to teach at Spokane Community College. John Prideaux asked me to replace him.

"I'm not a member," I said.

Prideaux paid my dues, and suddenly I was involved. I had only gone to three conventions because I saw them as just social events with only minor training value.

The best convention had been my first, in Vancouver, British Columbia, in 1964. The Canadian convention had been full of wild debate, and I was impressed.

I agreed with John on the condition that we tried to copy the Canadian format.

John Prideaux, Betty Winkler, Lynne Davis, and Judy Davis (not related) built on the Canadian model. Most of the past conventions had been in downtown areas to allow for shopping. We selected a motel in the valley for its isolation.

We scheduled debates and topics such as the Department of Corrections and the Juvenile Sentencing Reform Act, and those on each side set boundaries and debated. Our format created a buzz and we sold out.

We had a hot potato when the WCA board heard about our agenda—top WCA leaders were uneasy about sessions on separation from the DSHS, as the DSHS resisted such talk and did not want membership to vote on legislation.

But we moved forward. We had high standards of involvement and our sessions had a punch. Speakers did themselves proud.

Membership voted for the winners of the debates at the yearly business meeting.

When the votes were counted, the WCA board appointed a committee to write a Department of Corrections bill. WCA President Bridges resigned to take a federal parole board post, and Vice President Virginia Swanson became WCA president.

The WCA board hoped the issue would vanish but membership wanted two sessions in 1974 to write a bill for the fall. The sessions were taken over by the DSHS and held at the Echo Glen Juvenile Facility.

At the first committee session, I saw it was going nowhere. The talk was about costs or the confusion a bill would cause. The second meeting was canceled.

Time was short before the fall conference in Olympia. The conference was a training session, so there would be no debates. A bill would have to wait until the next year.

But my sense was that the DSHS or Governor Evans would end grass roots talk before then. If we had no bill, we would miss our chance. I recalled Commissioner Jerry Kopet once saying, "Don't ask a question unless you know the answer," and that nothing was over until you quit.

I had never written legislation, but with Kopet's words in mind I wrote a bill. I found Senate Bill 52, which had transferred field service to the Department of Institutions in 1967, and used it as a guide. I drafted a corrections bill during my weekends, and I sent a draft to friendly legislators in the House and the Senate. I heard nothing back, and I did not follow up.

As the previous conference's chair, my role at the Olympia session was to find a luncheon speaker. I selected Senator "Big Daddy" Day, from Spokane. Big Daddy was a character and had strong views on the DSHS as a political animal. I had no clue as to Daddy's goals, but he was a newsmaker in the legislature.

I heard that no bill would surface, yet in November 1974, House Bill 77 was in my home mailbox. Legislators in the House and Senate had picked up on what I had sent and written a proper bill, which they filed with the code office. For my part, as a state employee I did not lobby. I kept my mouth shut.

While waiting for further legislative action, I was contacted by an FBI agent. Elize, a parolee who had died near Forks, Washington, had just been arrested in Denver, Colorado. Elize had threatened to kill Nixon as the president campaigned in Denver.

The FBI said a person with Elize's identification had fallen from the cliff near Forks. The FBI had now committed Elize to a mental hospital in Colorado. I notified the parole board.

* * *

At the 1974 WCA Christmas party there was a brief session for members. I handed out copies of House Bill 77 and Senate Bill 77, both of which had been filed with the code reviser. Surprisingly, both bills reflected my input almost word for word. With the draft in hand, the board voted its support. HB 77 passed quickly in the next House session.

Senator Day held back SB 77 as a trading chip until Governor Evans broke the logjam by issuing an executive order creating a Division of Corrections within the DSHS, effective July 1, 1975. The legislature was generally satisfied and the Senate bill died in committee.

I was also satisfied with the results. I felt we had refocused on criminal justice and the corrections mission. I wanted peace and quiet after five years under DSHS control.

But one thing was for sure—the 1970 vision of corrections would not return after five years of regional influence and reorganization. Under the DSHS a paradigm shift had occurred in the state. Leadership wanted the WSP mess off the daily front pages. Institutions and work release had become points of emphasis and I predicted no turning back of the clock.

Governor Evans's effort to disempower federal agencies had shifted funding into the DSHS. His effort had occurred as the California drug craze spilled into Washington, and prison populations mushroomed as a result.

Regional citizens' advisory boards recommended policies to supercede locally delivered services in favor of state solutions that would cut across regions. Yet multi-service delivery centers did not focus on public protection as a priority.

A go along to get along attitude had spread, so probation varied from region to region. The supervision culture had been severely weakened.

The DSHS had pledged local choice, but keeping funding decisions in Olympia had ensured failure, which in turn spawned conspiracy theories and talk of guerrilla tactics. The egg of justice had been broken, and field service's functions were spilled yolk.

* * *

The penitentiary was still out of control—inmates lived in hell because the DSHS had no corrections background. Managers did not know when to cut their losses. The rule in the WSP was there were no rules, merely raw power obtained through fear tactics.

No price was too high to keep power. Members of the resident government council, an inmate-elected body that was part of Conte's rehabilitation scheme on the Hill, began to use their position to strong-arm other prisoners. Combat between groups and clubs was the norm and chilled any hopes of self-governance.

There were eighteen dead inmates in eighteen months at the WSP. Washington had no death penalty, but Blood Alley ran red. The public, once in the dark, awoke and demanded to know how to stop the bleeding in cellblocks.

I was liaison to a governor's task force at the WSP and assumed it was known that I was a source to Prosecutor Don Brockett. On site, I found that was not true. I was expected to support Evans's kitchen cabinet of executives, elected officials, and superior court judges.

We spent three days on the Hill and two days downtown. King County Judge Reveille and the group assessed the Hill and reported to Evans. I became very aware of penitentiary and town politics.

I sat near the back wall, off to one side, as witnesses answered sharp queries on the first day. I saw a lack of candor, meaning no real issues were discovered. It seemed that Bobby Rhay, prison staff, and RGC members were trying to hoodwink the committee.

On day two I saw more frustration. At midday the task force stopped and asked for a tour. RGC members gave a tour inside.

It was an in-your-face walk. We saw what the RGC wanted us to see. The timing of our tour took inmates by surprise, and we received a wide berth. We saw dirt, felt fear, and heard yelling. I saw quick flashes of anger on the faces of the governor's staff. I thought Evans would get a report in which members said, "I cannot believe this." But I could.

On day three we toured minimum-security, south of the main prison. The building was clean and staff was clearly in control. The contrast was stark—inmates mingled freely and spoke of their fear of the inside.

Staff members were upbeat and the inmates worked. The space was quiet. Task force members looked at each other, recalling the noises of the day before. I wondered what they were thinking.

Rhay wrapped up our tour with his standard talk on penitentiary history. He showed no frustration but I was sure he felt strongly—he read people well and knew his career was short.

Much would have to happen before staff could take control again. I knew any attempt to retake the penitentiary would be difficult, a task that would require hard work and commitment.

On day four we met in a motel conference room with local officials who were upbeat. Their mood surprised the task force members. Town folk were not concerned and supported Rhay. The local officials focused solely on money issues.

I had forgotten how blind locals were to the realities of the Hill. During our meeting they spoke of impact monies for both the superior court and the sheriff. We noticed how little officials and citizens cared about newspaper stories in Seattle or Spokane.

Our meeting ended early but a final session was to occur later in Seattle. Questioned briefly, I confirmed that local citizens had no interest. I heard nothing further. Perhaps there was no final report.

In any case Evans now knew that the DSHS lacked the capacity to deal with penitentiary trouble, and he was on the hook for the problems on the Hill.

* * *

In 1974 Evans hired Lloyd Patterson from California to implement major changes. At the time corrections was full of issues and trying to live out multiple philosophies and balance morality and reality.

Change is normal in crime and punishment. It is driven by resources, civic values and fears, and politics.

The Washington Territory was established in 1853, and for two decades punishment was by whipping post and lash. Serious crimes called for a rope and tree. By the 1870s, most counties had their own jails. Hudson's Bay Jail had been built at Steilacoom, Washington, in 1853. In 1874 a private prison was built at Seatco, south of Olympia.

Two stories high and made of wood, Seatco housed ninety-three inmates, three to a cell. Washington Territory paid the prison owners seventy cents daily per inmate. Prisoners were forced to work in logging, coalmines, a sawmill, or a barrel factory, with the owners keeping the profits of their labor. Seatco was shut down when the Washington Territory penitentiary in Walla Walla opened in 1887. In 1890 the federal government offered their prison on McNeil Island to the state of Washington for $36,000.

From 1897 to 1921, the Board of Audit and Control was the local trustee at the WSP. In 1908 the state reformatory was built in Monroe. In 1921, prison responsibilities were shifted to the Department of Business Control and Efficiency. A newly formed Division of Parole and Transportation took over operation of prisons in 1926.

In 1935, parole duties were moved to the Office of Financial Management, and by 1947 the Department of Institutions was running state hospitals and prison facilities.

Garrett Heynes was director of the Department of Institutions from 1957 until 1965. Dr. William Conte succeeded him and in 1967 Dr. Conte assumed control of probation and parole from the Board of Prison Terms and Paroles.

Prior to the birth of the Department of Social and Health Services in 1971, Larry Delmore had run the prison division within the Department of Institutions for fourteen years. The first secretary of the DSHS, Sidney Smith, lasted less than three years. Randy Rathfelder and Milton Burdman were both acting secretary in 1973.

The DSHS went through Division of Prisons leaders in a hurry. Tom Pinnock served a year in 1972. Dan Jensen then worked for seven months before Robert Tropp held the position for a year. In 1974, Lloyd Patterson was acting corrections director until Hal Bradley arrived. Leadership changes complicated operations and baffled citizens.

Cabinet managers in corrections lived a gypsy life, constantly turning over as a sort of heat shield for the governor. When a governorship ended it meant a change was likely in corrections leadership. Reform came in many shapes: technologies, buildings, law changes, and reorganizations.

New construction showed a tangible effort by leadership, creating few headaches while providing visible progress and creating jobs.

Staffers also liked toys and equipment, and if they were bought with federal grants, no legislative action was necessary. Hence technology was always in the pipeline. The leadership philosophy was, if you want to please staff easily, buy stuff.

Reorganizations and new legislation were riskier efforts. Life could get messy if careers were at stake. Agency consolidations brought chaos.

Crime issues were the pesky flies at the political garden party, unpleasant to talk about because they were interwoven with economics.

* * *

Land developers and local governments supported new buildings with impact fees. To justify the cost, leaders suggested that building prisons would cut crime. It was not true, but it earned the public's support.

There are in fact valid reasons to build new prison facilities, i.e., inmate safety and health, but the reality is prisons do not deter crime. Crooks do not plan to be arrested and, in truth, 72 percent are not. Most people who are arrested are young or under the influence of drugs or alcohol.

Forget prisons; we can better deter crime by giving people guidance, a chance to grow while being mentored by law-abiding adults. Why do we hurt each other?

I argue that if you give children a good family, good schooling, and good peers, then with luck or church values or both, they do okay. But if one of those goods is missing, bad things can happen.

Courts must not merely release folks who seriously hurt people, so we do need prisons. However, we must recognize that the recidivism rate doubles after serving time in prison.

* * *

Initially the DSHS responded to regional users of services, so market forces shaped each region's services. Non-profits and city or county agencies saw revenue from contracts, and with these complexities and soft audits locals bought into regional type services. Life varied depending on who was regional manager. In all the uncertainty staff members lacked a mission and had to fight for some kind of identity.

Lloyd Patterson, who headed the corrections division within the DSHS in 1974, asked for updated policies; he wanted a paper trail to hold both staff and inmates accountable. In corrections a paper trail also provides clean audits. Yet it does no good if staffers are not motivated once they are hired.

We saw rolling reorganizations four times between the summers of 1969 and 1980 with staff energy put into integrating five agencies, then into an unworkable ten regions concept. The DSHS later dropped to six regions, and eventually the Division of Corrections was created. Field staffers were afterthoughts in regional organization, only linked by the title probation and parole. The spotlight on prisons caused field services' slow death. Field services never totally reconnected to Olympia.

Layers of committees handcuffed by regulations dealt with issues at the penitentiary. Dr. Conte finally hit a hornets' nest and left in 1971. Patterson started to take back control of the Hill, but it would be years in the doing.

In Spokane, Bob Lizee took a demotion from regional administrator to parole and probation officer to avoid the ongoing stress. Prideaux replaced him, but later gave up the post so Bob could reassume his job; it was an unusual act of loyalty.

Milton Burdman became acting secretary of the Department of Social and Health Services again in 1974. He preceded and followed Charles Morris. Burdman hired Mr. Hal Bradley as director of corrections.

Left to Right: Ike Morrison, Hal Bradley, Bill Reilly and John Heffernan 1979

Bradley saw prisons as front-page news; the penitentiary had consumed the DSHS. Bradley wanted breezeways and cellblocks controlled and assaults stopped. But large prisons change very slowly, so Hal's long-term solution was smaller regional prisons he called mini-prisons.

With Governor Evans's support, Bradley created a prison siting task force. The mini-prison plan was implemented regionally but work release stayed centralized. Field staff now reported to Olympia. But the regions had grown apart, and it took much effort to bring staff together. Old divides existed between rural and urban, and east and west, as the effects of the DSHS culture lingered.

Sergeant Ike Morrison was county work release director and received an LEAA grant to build a separate WR entrance at the jail. Cameras allowed master control to monitor the entrance to WR. Work release needed space, so I moved to the S & T Building on Broadway across from the courthouse.

I was no longer working above the staff, which helped me break old habits. I felt pressure from Olympia to separate from the jail; they wanted me to site and run a unit for state inmates only. I resisted. I believed diversion was the best option, as it cut prison commitments.

Geiger Corrections Center
1979–1983

My opinions were not shared in Olympia, and I was ordered to find a location for a state work release facility. Pressure from headquarters built so I complained over coffee to Lieutenant Larry Erickson. Larry showed me the Geiger location in May 1974. Geiger had once been an air force base, but the buildings were gone except for two barracks, a chow hall, and a utility building. Spokane International Airport, co-owned by Spokane County and the City of Spokane, owned Geiger and planned to make it an industrial park.

Geiger's size was a shock, so I revisited it. I evolved a plan to use one barracks for work release and the second barracks for minimum-custody state or county inmates. Trustees would work in food service or do onsite work before being granted work release. When jail Captain Byron Franz retired, his replacement opposed the jail's use of volunteers and group meetings, so I lost the in-jail screening program.

I tried to sell the idea of Geiger to Olympia but found no interest there. Those who saw it thought I was nuts. I felt that Geiger could divert offenders and cut commitments to prison, yet that plan did not fly at headquarters.

Spokane County Sheriff William Reilly asked the county corrections department to run both the jail and the work release program, but corrections department directors Jim Flynn and Ray Mueller said no. When Joe Allen replaced Mueller as director in 1977 he accepted the work release program's transfer to county corrections. He assigned Don Linke as WR director. Joe showed support for my Geiger plan but he later said he didn't want to move to Geiger and showed an interest only to have an excuse to visit Seattle and have a good time. He did not want to back Geiger; he believed the state would soon seek to control it.

Geiger slipped to the back burner until Joe Allen resigned in 1978 and Don Linke became corrections director. Bud Quackenbush, an attorney for the airport, worked behind the scenes for Geiger and talked to the airport's board members and to the FAA.

Quackenbush saw issues with security, transportation, sewer, and water. He used these obstacles as reasons to support the Geiger concept—we would bring transportation, sewer, and water infrastructure into Spokane's west plains. Geiger became a reality only because of Bud's hard work.

My Geiger effort caught Hal Bradley's attention in 1975 as he was working on mini-prisons. He had divided the state into three regions, with each to receive its own prison. I became the eastern Washington regional liaison.

* * *

Probation and parole was effective but Olympia kept quiet about its success. Field services, as an alternative to prison, stayed hidden below citizens' radar. Probation was not a clearly defined term statewide, nor did it have an effective voice.

King County Prosecutor Chris Bayley brought up issues with the parole board—specifically, no one was pursuing efforts at diversion or new local programs. Field staffers felt justified. The prison leaders who set state policy were only focused on what started at the prison door.

Olympia had allowed work release units to operate on a don't ask, don't tell policy. Managers had very different views on what worked. In Spokane we were structured and stressed diversion efforts. We had close ties to field personnel and police. In Seattle and Tacoma, WR was simply a re-entry program for inmates from state prisons.

I learned quickly that Hal Bradley disliked recycled buildings; he wanted a new 144-bed mini-prison. Bradley knew that Northern State Hospital had converted old buildings into the Firland Corrections Center in 1975. Robert Kastama was Firland's first superintendent.

A mini-prison, once sited, could grow to deal with prison overcrowding. It was easier for a small prison to grow than to find a site for a new prison. I had marching orders and all other options were off the table.

The mini-prison plan set conditions such as access to utilities, suppliers, and the labor pool. In my statements I stressed the beneficial impact of prison jobs in communities.

The mini-prison project was underway when Kathy gave birth to our son Jason on October 8, 1975. My days were busy, but nothing compared to Kathy's at home with five children age seven or younger. She worked day and night, and Jason did not sleep through the night for nearly a year.

My task force members were from east of the Cascades. They found two sites, one in Medical Lake and a second in Yakima. Hayworth and Anderson Inc. wrote an environmental review and final report. The firm did good work, so we finished in time to have sites approved by the 1977 legislative session.

The corrections division benefited from Hal's work getting public support for a prison, yet general prison struggles continued. A newspaper article ran a picture of the eighteen inmates killed at the WSP since 1971. The task forces in west side regions fell short. Bradley had misjudged resistance in the northwest and southwest of the state, and the west-side mini-prison idea died in the legislature.

* * *

Governor Dixy Lee Ray took office in January 1977. Dixy Ray's arrival was a watershed event—she was a penny pincher, conservative, liked recycled buildings, and often made snap decisions. Her stance forced Bradley to shift his attention to the vacant buildings at Eastern State Hospital.

Dixy Lee Ray stopped pushing to break up the DSHS even though it had been her campaign promise. She believed a breakup would be too costly.

Olympia again asked me to find a stand-alone work release building. Once more I suggested Geiger, but at the same time major incidents occurred in Seattle, Everett, and Tacoma's work release facilities and Olympia backed off on moving WR from the jail.

In 1977, Bradley and I toured Eastern State Hospital's campus. One building was a maximum-security unit that housed primates from the University of Washington medical school. On Pine Street was Pine Lodge, which once had housed a women's mental patient unit but was now used as storage.

Hal asked if I wanted the Pine Lodge superintendent post. I said no, because I preferred to keep working on Geiger. Tom Rolfs, the mini-prison task force's state liaison, was named superintendent of Pine Lodge instead. He had worked at the Washington Corrections Center in Shelton.

The Pine Lodge building was unheated and full of stored junk. I doubted a remodel would work, even if it was gutted to bare brick, but that was not my worry. Penitentiary inmates were sent to clean Pine Lodge for construction, housed by Spokane WR. Their work took ninety days, during which I continued to work on Geiger as a solution to jail crowding.

The cleanup crews had a supervisor to transport them, and they left before breakfast and returned after dinner. The crew was allowed to eat in a restaurant if they did a good day's work. Inmates worked hard to avoid jail food and finished the cleaning ahead of schedule. Construction started in April 1977.

I saw Tom Rolfs occasionally during construction. He was hiring and training staff. Kurt Peterson, who had a strong personality, was hired as the associate superintendent.

Don Linke and I spoke to county commissioners about jail relief. I wrote to the FAA regarding Geiger just as Bud Quackenbush requested; he was quietly on a mission, and things suddenly started to change.

Regional Administrator Bernie Nelson said that Geiger qualified for Referendum 29 funds, which would provide one million dollars in capital. The next day Spokane County installed a fence at Geiger to prevent vandalism. State and county officials signed a ten-year contract for state inmate beds in Building B. After four years, Geiger was showing signs of life.

* * *

WCA membership in Spokane was energetic for WCA President John Prideaux, who wanted to tell the story of corrections to the public. WCA members developed a television show that reported on criminal justice in the state. Project director Patricia Scott documented local justice cooperation and held town hall meetings at Gonzaga University. I was pleased that local probation and parole staff had decided to tell their story to the general public.

Our effort took seven weeks to look at police, prosecution, defense, judges, probation, prisons, and the parole board. Governor Ray even provided her input on tape.

The show aired on KREM, with help from Gonzaga University, Eastern Washington University, the League of Women Voters, the Spokane Bar Association, the Spokane Chamber of Commerce, the Junior League, the Washington Commission for the Humanities, the Comstock Foundation, the Kiwanis Clubs of Spokane, and architect John McGough.

Tapes of the project were archived in the state library in Olympia.

* * *

I had turned down a job at Pine Lodge Corrections Center (PLCC), but ironically I ended up working there anyway, only with Rolfs as my boss instead of the other way around.

In June 1977, Superintendent Bobby Rhay was relieved of his duties at the WSP. Douglas Vinzant was assigned to the post in October 1977. Shortly thereafter, Dixy Ray fired Hal Bradley for objecting to the use of old buildings for prison housing.

Newly minted WSP Superintendent Douglas Vinzant replaced Bradley as director of corrections. He stayed at the penitentiary hoping to arrive in Olympia as the hero of the prison wars, but the trouble on the Hill kept going. Doug was stuck in Walla Walla as the legislature began its session in January 1978.

Unable to be in two places at once, Doug became a scapegoat. The con bosses knew he would not leave under a cloud; people would say the inmates ran him out of town.

Vinzant, not a patient man, was frustrated. After one incident, Vinzant called the con bosses into a conference room and fired a shotgun blast at a trashcan on the table. The gun was loaded with a lead slug, not a rubber slug as he believed. The slug ripped into the trashcan and through a wall into the business manager's office. Luckily the manager was not at his desk.

Reports of the shooting arrived in Olympia with Doug and he was called Dead Eye, not exactly considered the hero he had hoped to be.

Doug was later fired from both his positions after a lighter bomb blew up at the WSP, killing a staff member. Jim Spalding replaced him as superintendent and locked down the penitentiary, but the news spotlight was still focused on the DSHS as if it was a bad dream. The DSHS had hoped to cut its losses when it formed the Division of Corrections, yet it could not distance itself from corrections goofs.

Legislators began to look beyond the DSHS, and seeds were sown for a complete review of Washington's criminal code. Citizens were aware that the parole board had reduced some ten- or twenty-year terms to eighteen months or two years. There was civic pressure to make set terms more visible.

* * *

The remodeling of Geiger started in June 1978. Resistance to the project had vanished after more troubles at the penitentiary. Pine Lodge opened September 17, 1978, and Geiger was planned to be its satellite. I reported to Tom Rolfs and attended weekly PLCC meetings.

The meetings became on-the-job training sessions on running an institution. PLCC had opened as a medium-security facility with eighty-five beds. Inmates were housed in four open dorms. A twelve-foot fence surrounded the housing; at dusk, armed security staff walked the perimeter.

East of the main PLCC compound were the vacant Lake View Apartments overlooking Medical Lake. Later the apartments would house a twenty-bed work release program. My PLCC duties were limited, but I pushed for inmate jobs at Eastern State Hospital and Lakeland Village.

I watched Rolfs face issues in the self-contained community. His life was complicated. In contrast, with my veteran staff downtown, WR was running on autopilot. Tom Rolfs did not stay long at PLCC—he was promoted to director of correctional industries in Olympia in early 1979.

Peggy Hoffman was named PLCC superintendent that July. She was the first female superintendent of a male prison in Washington. In our first meeting she told me that Geiger would be free-standing. I would not report to her, but to Dick Vernon, the deputy director of prisons.

My time at Pine Lodge taught me not to get ahead of line staff. I had discovered some of the things I lacked, and knew that I would have to hire experienced personnel. I would need staff input to run a smooth operation at Geiger.

* * *

Geiger's barracks were built in 1952, and our remodel was largely cosmetic. We added new electronic security and electronic control rooms. We built holding cells in each of the housing units. Stops were added to the windows so a person would have to break glass in order to climb out. We put cameras on the perimeter to scan the eight-foot fence, which was monitored from both control rooms.

We installed a state-of-the-art kitchen and feeding line, and built a monitored recreation center and a classroom on either side of the dining hall. We added cameras in the hallways to monitor housing and exit doors.

There was major work in the boiler room. It had been flooded and needed an upgrade. Repairs were also made to a wood utility building that had once been an airman's club. A loaned military field kitchen reheated jail food for two months before our on-site kitchen was ready.

In May 1979 I was promoted to superintendent of Geiger. Work release opened that August with 160 work release beds in Building A, which doubled local WR beds. In December, ninety inmates moved into Building B. Our goal was to draw down the penitentiary population yet keep a lid on Geiger.

People in Olympia did not fully understand our diversion process and felt Geiger was a poor use of state resources. I ignored those feelings as I focused on the transition to Geiger, which was fairly easy—we simply moved existing work release operations from the jail. However, the size of Geiger was an adjustment from day one. I walked the site daily to comprehend its size.

The absence of jail scenery improved offenders' performance and behavior. We emphasized employment through five-day-a-week job searches. In the interest of public safety we had simple rules with strict boundaries, and 92 percent of residents kept to the limits.

I felt we had made it. Geiger was open. National media said Geiger was a great example of how local and state agencies could work together to lower costs.

Co-management in the justice arena between counties and the state required a lot of trust. Geiger existed only because we had built that trust. Trust could only grow if we kept things simple, so we avoided complexities and complications; we shared and trusted.

* * *

At Geiger I applied what I had seen and learned at Pine Lodge and knew I was lucky I had not taken the prior job offer. If I had accepted the PLCC superintendent position, I would have been dead meat. Instead I had had time to watch Tom make routine decisions.

Tom ran his institution with custody restrictions and limited options. A clear line separated the kept and the keepers. Staffers did not openly express their needs in Tom's command and control environment—they simply took orders. The tradeoff was that staffers left independent thinking at the door. I, on the other hand, required my staff to think.

I empowered people with choice to encourage learning and growth. I also supported inmates' development in their decision-making. My ideas were foreign at PLCC. I spent my days selling my ideas to county or state staff, but no one questioned Tom.

The military mindset was top-down, so the chain of command was captains, lieutenants, sergeants, and line officers. A superintendent had more power than I had in work release. Tom set the tone for Pine Lodge. I had tried to avoid power conflicts there; I was an outsider who was just there to give input.

PLCC Associate Superintendent Kurt Peterson, with his military experience, had issues when Peggy Hoffman installed a therapeutic program at PLCC. Peggy's program meant staff listened, cared, and responded to inmates with kindness. Kurt transferred at his first opportunity.

When I started hiring staff for Geiger, I went to Pine Lodge for experienced people. Peggy was open to my interest, as she could then hire or promote staffers who shared her beliefs as she refilled positions at Pine Lodge.

* * *

Though hopes were high with the creation of the corrections division of the DSHS in 1975, the need for prison beds consumed the 1970s. By 1980 the new Department of Corrections had arrived with more effective leadership—people who recognized that the current WR system lacked vision and instead pushed to centralize work release.

The WR landscape in the 1980s was a mixed bag. We operated in prisons, slum housing, old hotels, and jails. We accepted questionable inmates to control prison overcrowding. Working across the state from the capitol meant more freedom—WR managers sidestepped the parole board's questions and our success rates slipped. Operational support from Olympia was minimal.

I saw WR as a tool for field staff to structure the use of community supervision. We were most effective when we worked together, as departmental conflict took the focus off offenders' performance. I wanted teamwork so I hired staff with solid backgrounds and people skills, people who would say what they meant and mean what they said.

Delegation and good communication were paramount in running an institution; control disintegrated when staffers ignored small issues.

It was a busy time, and what went unnoticed were the waves of reform building in Seattle and Olympia.

One issue on the table was court discretion. There were committees on sentencing and lack of transparency of prison terms.

Prisons were in the headlines and holding citizens' attention. The number of crimes overwhelmed the wary public, and citizens looked to judges or the parole board for a solution to the rising crime issues in the news. But no quick fix existed.

* * *

I reported to Dick Vernon, the deputy director of prisons, which was a big deal to me because I had not reported to a deputy director before. But to him I was a minor concern; he had larger fish to fry and could not hold my hand.

I butted heads with Vernon over the size of my staff. I wanted to limit staff size so that county and state staffers would have to work together. Dick said that Building B was a stand-alone unit.

I replied, "Geiger, to be effective, must operate as a single unit."

Dick consented but said, "Don't knock at my door later for added staff. That will not happen. Do you get my point?"

I did. Vernon caused me to rethink my position, so I took two of the six staff positions he offered. I left the positions vacant for off-site work crew supervisors. We stayed simple and lean, and that reality dictated that staff had to work together to avoid a them vs. us mentality.

With months to go I realized I did not know how to staff Geiger, so I hired to cover my weaknesses and did it quickly. I sought mature staff with good work histories—the best and brightest.

My interviews were informal; I took one-on-one walks with candidates and asked questions about what to do here or there. I wanted staffers who could think on their feet.

I hired managers to run counseling, food services, business management, and custody. Work release was already working, but I needed managers who knew their field, my goals, and would work effectively with county staff. Once hired, I played the role of their student as they educated me on their duties.

I hired Bob Enright for WR supervisor, an easy choice. He had volunteered with me at the jail and already knew county staff. Bob was the kind of detailed person that I was not. His reputation was as a blue-collar worker who was not afraid to call a spade a spade. With Bob working, I could focus on being superintendent.

I tried to steal Lieutenant Danny Walker from PLCC, but he turned me down. Sergeant Al Ramos was my next choice for lieutenant. He had worked at the penitentiary and on Pine Lodge's startup team. He knew the prison culture, our equipment, and supply needs. He could do audits and write manuals and post orders, which listed a staffer's duties and how to do them.

Al was young, but gave clear answers to questions about hiring custody staff. My concern was whether he could deal with county staff. Ron Myers was the county's Geiger director and also interviewed my candidates. He approved Al Ramos because he liked Al's penitentiary experience.

Tana Wood was a candidate for program manager. She was a social worker and a counselor at the reception unit at the Washington Corrections Center in Shelton. Tana supported installing unit teams for inmate interaction instead of individual counselors, but my plate was too full at startup and I felt county staff would object. Tana knew about classification and was detail oriented, so she would be able to move inmates through the system, as Geiger was a 60- to 90-day housing unit.

Tana would also push the rest of my staff to improve Geiger. She was an inmate advocate, offsetting Al's security bent. She was hard driving, with networks of contacts statewide. She was upset that I rejected her unit team idea, but agreed that we must do first things first. Tana met with Ron and he gave her a lukewarm approval. Myers was concerned that Tana was pushy.

I hired Don Gaumer as food manager after a walk around the Geiger kitchen. Don had run field kitchens in Vietnam and various officers' clubs. He knew food service and was a jewel. Don talked about starting a cooking and baking school, so he had Myers's total support. Ron saw Gaumer as my best hire because Ron had served in Vietnam and valued good food.

I hired Jim Fox as business manager but he had little experience in accounting; he was one exception to the experience rule. Myers had no interest in Jim, but Fox was eager, listened, and showed a real willingness to help. I had seen business managers run programs by controlling allotments, and I did not want that attitude at Geiger.

At PLCC, I had learned I would need to understand my budget, that it must be transparent with all allotments visible. Jim learned with me as I learned the budget.

My second exception to the experience rule was June Dalzell, my former secretary at WR in the S & T Building. I recognized her past help and hired her as records officer. It was a big career move for strong-willed June. She was not a diplomat and I needed a softer image and communicator at Geiger, so I hired Judy Ross as my administrative assistant. She was effective, organized, and paid attention to detail. Judy cleaned up my letters and reports.

Judy gave straight answers yet did not try to control any of my decisions. She took shorthand, so I could dictate reports and see the results properly formatted and in English.

With the Geiger slots filled, my job was to stay clear and support my staff. I set goals, but managers were accountable for their unit's operation. To maintain common direction, I held weekly briefings to hear managers' plans. This kept me informed and allowed me to ask general questions. After meetings, I wrote a summary and checked on the results.

I tested program and support options to ensure we were addressing our mission. I knew that in Olympia there were doubters, and I wanted to avoid ending up as road kill in Olympia.

* * *

At times we struggled. Don Gaumer did not like others in his kitchen. Al Ramos followed the book and could get moralistic and reactionary, but he was 110 percent committed. Tana often sided with inmates. She was headstrong and impatient and disliked delays; she wanted to get things right the first time. Fox lacked experience and the ability to say no, which could cause confusion on payday if he was off on payroll. Jim improved once he hired an accountant and bookkeeper.

Bob Enright ran state work release and tried to stay out of Building B's business. Myers's staff liked Bob, so he was my bridge. He worked daily with county staff, and Myers would talk to Bob before he brought up issues. Bob settled Myers down, but he would rather not have been in the middle.

There was a lot of turnover at Geiger, so we created a badge system for identification. Work release IDs had a blue background, inmates' were red, and staffers' were white. Visitors wore a white visitor badge. The badges allowed us to quickly identify who was who and if someone was out of bounds.

Under Al and Tana's leadership, arrivals were assigned work on their first day. Chain buses arrived on Wednesdays and each inmate was classified by Friday.

New arrivals lacking a high school diploma went to GED classes four nights each week. The classes were optional for work release, but we emphasized that reviewing English or math might help them to enter school later.

Spokane Community College teachers taught a job course for residents. These classes were mandatory for inmates who were not employed. State inmates could attend if slots were open.

Inmates worked eight hours a day. If an inmate refused to work, he was transferred without exception. Compulsory work set the tone and kept inmates busy. Work routines helped inmates see beyond the big house and transition into work release or parole. Work also helped inmates forget Walla Walla.

The largest employer was our kitchen and the grounds crew. One crew of ten inmates worked offsite for the airport board.

Clean dorms were a major statement that we were in control, and inmates who worked in housekeeping trained their replacements to our standards. Once training was completed, those inmates could move on to new jobs.

West side transfers had access to a job coach. Doug Huigen, from Trend Inc., helped inmates who were transferring to Seattle or Tacoma.

Huigen called employers to assess their needs and matched inmates to companies. By faithfully serving employers, Doug developed a satisfied group of businesses willing to hire inmates. Still, the newspaper and the yellow pages were his most useful tools.

* * *

We were a staging depot with simple rules, a place where inmates could refocus. We directed their thinking away from prison and toward work and school. Our template required work and simple discipline.

Major infractions meant a transfer out for ninety days, then an inmate could return to Geiger. Olympia's classification system did not like to deal with transfers, but we did not get to screen who came into Geiger and we did not want to run a zoo. My hard line kept animals out of Geiger so we could focus offenders on moving beyond prison.

A ninety-day return was a rejection of conduct, not the individual. Inmates had control over their custody—all they had to do was not assault others, drink, use drugs, try to escape, or refuse work. We held everyone accountable to our standard.

The idea was that if an offender didn't want to walk the walk, there were a hundred inmates at the penitentiary who did. That self-screening idea created a positive, fear-free environment.

By late 1979, inmates were arriving weekly. Monthly county-state meetings addressed site strengths, weaknesses, and team building. I walked one-on-one with managers each week to learn their agendas. I wanted the workplace to be open and sharing. I vowed to avoid unintended consequences that could surprise everyone.

During our first year, my biggest weakness was I was not sure what to expect. Yet somehow my staff carried Geiger. My strength was that I knew I did not know, so I asked questions, which focused staff.

Our cooking and baking school, drapery classes, and the job orientation class all evolved from staff suggestions. We shared ideas, worked smarter rather than harder, and kept processes simple. We gained momentum, but reality soon chimed in. Surprisingly, the DSHS days were, for me, the happy days at Geiger.

* * *

I awaited our first escape attempt and wondered how staffers would handle it. There had been many escapes at Pine Lodge, which had spawned negative press. The first priority of a custody unit was to keep inmates safe and in custody.

In the first two months we had no escapes. No one failed to return from work. That was uncommon in our business, so Tana Wood and Al Ramos tried to prepare staff for the inevitable. In the third month, on a cold January night, an escape occurred in early morning. The runner was a nineteen-year-old on kidney dialysis.

If Chad's escape was a success, he could die within days—he needed dialysis to live. He was depressed about his health, which kept him from work release. We found him in the weeds just yards from our unit. His escape was a wake-up call that we had no effective plan in place.

We drew up protocols to keep staff engaged so they would not overreact. We did not lock down Geiger after head count—that would just punish the inmates who stayed.

Geiger was near an airport runway and next door to a military housing unit. Al studied the airport map for exits. The flight line to our west and the freeway to the east were natural containments, so escapees would have to travel either north or south.

Al set up posts to be manned during an escape so we could jump ahead of a fleeing inmate. We also hired a bloodhound service, built escape kits, and created call lists to notify local television, radio, and print media to limit negative coverage. County and state staffers were teamed together to avoid finger pointing.

Once an escapee was caught, we interviewed him to improve our understanding of escape routes. We looked for patterns and asked why, where, and how questions. We examined internal factors for a cause. One common reason was inmate-on-inmate violence, so I installed a no-tolerance rule on bullying or fighting. A confirmed threat resulted in transfer.

One major incident in 1980 tested our no-tolerance policy. A group of eighteen inmates acted as if they were at the WSP—they hazed an inmate with a snitch jacket.

We heard rumors of a plan to beat up the snitch, which would be a message that Geiger was unsafe. A chain bus had just delivered inmates, and after hearing the rumors I brought the bus back with deputies. Geiger's troublemakers were loaded up for the trip south. It was over, and inmates did not again test Geiger.

Olympia was concerned about my actions and wanted a report. My opening comment was that any riot at Geiger would have gotten it shut down.

* * *

The penitentiary held two thousand inmates. In late 1980 the federal court took action to put an end to overcrowding and violence at the WSP, and the penitentiary was placed under control of a federal special master and for a time operated under federal court rules. As issues played out at the penitentiary, new political forces grew while field operations just limped along. Geiger housed a few inmates who testified on the scope of the WSP problems in Spokane's federal court.

The Spokane courts' use of Geiger, and the number of probationers, had grown since 1979. Spokane County's felony commitments had dropped 20 percent as felons were diverted from prisons. Geiger was a local resource without fanfare.

Geiger housed just ninety inmates, plus two hundred WR residents, so inmates' conduct was always visible at Geiger. Inmates were classified in a straightforward manner according to needs, abilities, and behavior. Classification was an exercise in matching an inmate's abilities with local resources and needs. After an inmate completed a barracks cleaning assignment we listed the job slots available to him. The slots and programs were self-selected and limited only by availability and education required.

Inmates saw others on WR leave and return. They saw their friends walking the walk. Most inmates dropped their dangerous airs and posturing from the WSP because they simply weren't useful.

At Geiger we held dorm meetings with citizen volunteers in Buildings A and B. Four residents from each floor attended, plus two from the women's section. We met weekly in a classroom to hear issues and give answers in an effort to limit rumors.

After a meeting, representatives would return to their dorms with volunteers and discuss issues. The volunteers mentored and gave common sense advice to inmates while ensuring there was a channel for feedback.

The meetings resolved the mysteries of work release as we shared insights about jobs, transportation, and costs. We kept meetings straightforward so inmates would understand options and limits. We hoped our dialogue would cause inmates to look to the future.

* * *

Bud Langan was the extension program director at Community Colleges of Spokane and oversaw all of Geiger's education programs. He always wanted to know how he could be of more help.

Bud found ways to serve by supplying job developers, and with his help we ran fully employed. Bud and Don Gaumer were soul mates—together they created the modular and competency-based culinary arts program. The program was open entry and open exit to graduation or transfer.

Food service was a training lab where students learned to cook by preparing meals. They learned about sanitation, equipment use, inventory, food preparation, presentation, and service.

The modular training helped ease problems with a rotating population. The class was split into ten parts. Each segment was a stand-alone unit that let a student start anywhere. The class never had vacant chairs.

Bud's competency scheme let students advance depending on ability. Classes were six days a week, eight hours a day, with students earning college credit. Don received calls for students from all across Washington—word of mouth was a big resource for employers in the food industry.

He even had calls from county jails offering to house graduates, pay them a wage, and help them find work upon parole.

Bud also developed two fourteen-week courses that provided skills training and also outfitted dorm rooms with drapery and Venetian blinds.

* * *

Geiger empowered inmates who followed rules. Rapid turnover forced us to set short-term goals to keep inmates busy, which cut down escapes.

In 1980, Building B was renamed Geiger Pre-Release at Geiger Corrections Center. Pre-release was a new concept created in the American prison system.

I visited Dick Vernon and learned that I would report to Work Release Director Ray Messagee, who oversaw Tacoma Pre-Release at Western State Hospital and all state WR units.

I objected to the change. There was limited help from Olympia for WR units. Most were freestanding units with institutional procedures; Geiger no longer seemed to fit into WR. Vernon said his decision was final. I asked to see Corrections Director Tropp, who confirmed I would report to Messagee.

I had worked for Ray before so he himself was not my issue. The issue was Geiger was operating out of bounds according to Ray's rules, but he would not change operations so I stuck out like a sore thumb. Luckily Olympia was across the state and the DSHS never had its act together, but Olympia had the money and money talks, so eventually something had to give.

* * *

We slowly drew down the population at the penitentiary. Inmates worked and were civil. Yet my leadership style worried my staff because I did not give directives. I felt that authoritarian methods did not allow choice and created phony relationships, so I resisted command and control and instead promoted choice as part of our mission to empower staff and inmates.

I met with inmates on Friday mornings to hear their concerns. I wanted their views. I saw no risk in creating an inmate power base as Geiger's turnover inherently controlled the power structure.

Staff got nervous about my weekly visits, wondering if I would give away the farm. Others worried I might learn they were arbitrarily applying rules or that inmate life at Geiger differed depending on the staff on duty.

Infractions sometimes reflected the staff on duty more than inmate behavior. I passed any comments or impressions on to staff in general terms, and hearing my input seemed to affect staff behavior.

* * *

I was too busy in 1980 to pay attention to the gubernatorial race or its potential impact on corrections. John Spellman won the office of governor and formed a transition team, led by Amos Reed, that would separate the Department of Corrections (DOC) from the DSHS.

Reed came from a prison background and had made his name in North Carolina and Oregon. A previous review by Governor Ray had suggested that breaking up the DSHS would be too costly, so Amos Reed would have to find legislative votes to support the breakup. He put together silent brokers to achieve votes. One group wanted well-run prisons, another wanted punishment, and the last wanted sentencing reform.

In early December 1980 a letter arrived from Governor-elect Spellman's chief of staff. It read, "If you wish to be Geiger superintendent, please submit an application."

The superintendent post was an at-will position. I submitted my application and was chosen to stay on at Geiger.

In mid-December, at a leadership meeting, acting DSHS Secretary Jerry Thomas said that legislation splitting corrections off from the DSHS was near.

"This will make John Heffernan happy," he said.

The truth was, after Geiger opened, I was too busy to track the issue. We had lived ten years with the DSHS. I thought a split would be good for both the DSHS and corrections. I left the leadership meeting with a wide smile.

* * *

Amos Reed's résumé was full. As president of the American Correctional Association he had a reputation for speaking straight and bloodying the noses of his opposition. Amos was a born leader who knew public opinion and took control of a weak and confused agency.

I was surprised by his ability to give his stakeholders great influence while staying three steps ahead. He had no interest in community corrections—he was a prison man.

Reed wheeled and dealed during 1981 as bills were passed and the dust settled. Soon he had the votes to create a Department of Corrections. In July 1981 Reed supported a bill to overhaul Washington's sentencing scheme. It became known as the Sentencing Reform Act (SRA). Few staffers, myself included, understood that a paradigm shift had occurred.

Amos Reed hit the ground running. He installed his team by September 1981, helped by Governor Spellman. Reed eliminated corrections' dependency on the DSHS and staff loyal to the DSHS.

Reed satisfied punishment and fair sentencing folks by playing a major role in the SRA, which adjusted the lengths of felony terms. The adjustments eliminated the judges' role in applying justice.

Sentencing options vanished, as did the Board of Prison Terms and Paroles' role of setting and adjusting prison terms.

The Washington Council on Crime and Delinquency established what they considered to be a fair sentencing process that removed staff bias from justice. Human factors in earlier sentencing models were now plotted on a weighted matrix, and legislators created a grid of crimes divided into three categories. Prior convictions changed where an accused person fell on this grid in terms of severity. The formula was based on a prosecutor's charges and did not consider other factors.

A term, once set, could not be adjusted except by a governor's emergency action to cut the terms of all low-end felons. To add sugar to the changes all initial terms for minor crimes were cut. The SRA did allow legislators to revisit the length of terms as needed, but cutting terms did not make political sense, so terms were increased as citizens sought to stop crime.

Prison intake slowed as field services shifted their focus to post-release cases and the number of probationers dropped. Probation and parole staffers became known as community corrections officers. Relationships with clients were now legalistic—we merely observed and reported.

I did not understand the reasoning behind the major sentencing changes. Why give up flexibility? Who was to say what sentence was proper for society's goals? If it wasn't a judge in public, it was a prosecutor behind closed doors who had power. And would SRA actually cut crime?

The effect of the SRA was that it initially lowered prison commitments, which was a windfall for Reed. His agency lacked beds, as few prisons had been built in the DSHS era and construction would take time. Reed was in a difficult spot, but with the drop in population on the Hill he regained some control. He later built a unit at Monroe and acquired the McNeil Island prison from the federal government.

* * *

Nineteen eighty-one started out as a quiet year as the DSHS withdrew and the new Department of Corrections was organized. On July 1, at the end of the 1980-81 biennial cycle, Reed's officials took over. With limited time to submit 1982-83 biennial numbers, I simply copied the prior budget, added inflation, and submitted it.

Headquarters was quiet as it built our agency's structure and hired for new positions. Memos started arriving from Olympia in November 1981, stressing prison needs and shifting budget allotments to prisons. Geiger was again a source of conflict as goals shifted.

Amos the brick and mortar man sought classification, good morale, and credibility. Sentencing reform was his ace in the hole to drop commitments. The determinate terms allowed solid predictions of future bed needs—someone could simply add up the number of sentenced people, multiply by the length of their terms, subtract releases, and come out with projected need.

The agency rule of thumb was to support Amos and mind your manners. He was folksy but had no shades of gray. I was not an insider, so I did not see his cold side. I heard that if a staff member arrived badly dressed, was unprepared, or tried to B.S. him, they quickly learned that Amos was the boss.

Reed increased prison capacity and imported managers, introducing them at statewide meetings. Amos, like his namesake the biblical prophet, had a mission. He was accountable to the citizens and the governor. He believed that the DOC's work began when an offender entered prison.

* * *

In 1981 I was busy, happy, and brain dead. Geiger was full and we had few surprises. With my team in place, all was right with the world. Yet gloom lay down the road that fall. I had not foreseen the impact of SRA on diversion. After 1981, talk of probation was muted; only the language of prisons was spoken within the agency.

I saw offenders as individuals and mixed pre- and post-SRA cases at Geiger. The Geiger project had been a partnership, yet the new administration felt that weak leadership had supported it. If Geiger had been on the table in 1981, it would not have happened.

Community Corrections Division Director Ross Peterson hired Bob Lippold as director for work release. Judy Smith was named director for field services.

Bob centralized work release operations. He left no doubt that he would shape work release policies and get results. He confronted staffers in meetings, including those from non-profits and public agencies. He was a hardnosed and in-your-face leader, not a listener.

I left my first meeting with Bob feeling that diversion would cause him problems. We were the largest unit in the state and had eight years left on our contract. Bob had power because Amos Reed said so, and Reed also knew Spokane County had become a powerful influence in Olympia.

* * *

Bob Lippold visited in September 1981 and I met him at his hotel room. He answered my knock wrapped in a towel. As Bob dressed he spoke of Utah and the Gary Gilmore execution by firing squad, which had happened on his watch. Bob had liked to talk with Gary and visited Gilmore as he awaited his execution.

Bob was a stocky man and a stylish dresser. He had energy and confidence and looked to be in his mid-forties.

We went outside, but at my state car he waved me off; we took his red sports car instead. We snaked out of the parking lot onto Trent Avenue. Bob drove with flair and had no need for brakes. I told him Trent was a one-way street, but he took no notice as we drove against traffic.

I realized that Bob made his own rules. He was laughing about the one-way street when we arrived at Geiger. He asked no questions and I had no idea what was on his mind. I let Bob take the lead.

My annoyance grew as he refused to sign in at security. He met WR Director Ron Myers, County Corrections Director Don Linke, and Leon Mayer. Bob ignored their greetings. He was a piece of work.

"Geiger was important but wrong," he told me. "I will change that."

He could not accept that county staff had the authority to deny inmate entrance to Geiger.

"That must be an Olympia decision," he said.

I walked behind him as we toured. County staffers were confused by his lack of interest—they had hoped to impress him. Halfway into the tour he said, "I've seen enough. I have other things to do."

We said our goodbyes to the staff and walked to my office. Bob sat at my desk and talked more about Utah.

"County folk are hicks," he said. "Set a date to reopen talks. The county will not screen inmates. That will stop."

Bob ignored my input that the site lease—by Spokane County from the airport board—called for screening and would not be changed.

Bob had no interest in visiting further with staff. He had to find a friend for lunch at the community corrections office on Broadway. He asked if I would show him the way.

On the drive downtown, I brought up the screening process again. I said, "You will lose that screening quarrel."

Bob said, "Don't worry. You are not part of the talks. You are part of the problem."

At the field office, Bob asked me if a blond secretary at the office dated.

"Her husband would object," I said.

Bob had a lunch date. He told me he was busy and said, "Find your way back to the car."

Bob's first visit was over. Winds of change had arrived.

* * *

I retrieved my state car and stopped at the courthouse to see Linke for feedback. I talked about standing firm on existing contract agreements.

"Bob is nuts," I said.

Don surprised me by saying, "The county talks, it's a good opportunity."

Recalling Geiger's history, I asked him to stand firm.

But Don said, "Talking with Bob is in our interest."

Don reopened Geiger talks. The choice cost him any future help from me. I was not involved when Don met with Lippold, yet I was the one who had to deal with new doubled bed costs in WR.

Bed rates strained our budget, and we faced cuts as state revenues dropped in 1982. It was my first try at making a budget, though I did have help from both Pine Lodge and Olympia in creating it. It was clear that budget drove policy and vice versa.

Budget cuts meant I had to do more with less, compared to smaller units. We operated both work release and a full custody unit. We were larger than Tacoma Pre-Release and all their business support was done free of charge by headquarters staff, while our business office worked on our dime.

Bob Lippold dropped his effort when the wheels fell off the wagon but he blamed me for the results. He cut costs to cover his failed negotiations and made the cuts retroactive to July 1981. A 10 percent retroactive cut amounted to 21 percent going forward. I said that it was unfair, but my concern went unheard. When I sat down to deal with the cuts, I found that the majority of my budget was staff, so it would be impossible to meet the new budget without layoffs.

We adjusted operations and limited inventories, but that was not enough. I asked to use our education money to pay staff instead, as tough times require solutions. The reply was no, and to show he was serious Bob ordered an audit of Geiger. Headquarters staff would ensure I made the proper cuts.

Bob asked DOC Budget Manager John King to read me the RCW for over-spending; a gross misdemeanor, the sanctions were a fine or jail. King was nervous. I sat at my desk. Bob, on the couch, clearly enjoyed the event. He was the cat and I the mouse.

When John finished I asked Bob to explain the intent behind the retroactive cuts.

"This is nuts," I said. "Put the RCW away and do your audit. We will cooperate."

Perhaps Bob felt an audit would reshape Geiger or put the last nail in my coffin by proving I could not manage the place.

My response was, "Get on with it. I want a complete audit. How long will it take?"

"Five days," he said.

* * *

The audit was easy. Geiger managers had experience answering questions. The audit team was in awe of Gaumer's inventory and access to navy dry dock foodstuffs. He bought quality items at a 90 percent discount. The sole negative the auditors saw was that our meals were too good. Citizens did not expect inmates to get Gaumer's level of quality, and they might complain.

"Good food cut our escape rate," I said. "No one wanted to miss a meal."

Tana Wood showed how she classified new arrivals within eight hours so that programming would start at orientation. Her unit reports were current and the files showed quality contacts. She was the big engine that kept our beds full via her relationship with the WSP. Soon after the audit Tana hired on at the penitentiary as associate superintendent.

Work release ran smoothly under Bob Enright. Staffers were involved in job searches and rarely failed. Bob's weekly meetings ensured a review of all residents. The audit teams considered the fact that we carried probation cases a negative.

Enright later transferred to a prison classification post in Olympia. I did not replace him or Tana, and Kerry Kirking assumed both duties. Kerry did not miss a beat even when WR officer Tim Foley transferred to the Broadway office.

Al Ramos's maintenance and housekeeping got high marks. Al documented offenders' training and his staff worked well with the county, so we had been able to cut staff on the graveyard shift. Our post orders were current and we used little overtime.

Business Manager Jim Fox was still learning—auditors found and noted mistakes. Yet King said that despite a lack of experience, Jim was learning quickly. Geiger's accounting work was below standards, but there was no misuse of funds.

Jim was faulted for letting Don Gaumer buy dry dock supplies. Even if Don's buys were legitimate, there were issues about local accounts. Normally units used the Olympia work release trust fund. Our work release unit did, but our pre-release unit used a local bank.

Work release's policy said we had to get approval for all purchases over $500. Fox had not followed that directive. The audit team said we needed a waiver to do what we were doing. I said I had Dick Vernon's waiver and told the auditors to check the files in Olympia.

Olympia's trust fund was another issue. Because of high turnover, we needed quick access to money. Banks in Olympia and the United States Postal Service did not meet our needs.

Lippold stayed for only two days. He lost interest once it was clear no major errors existed. King did the audit exit interview. He talked mostly about Jim Fox, our inventory of orange coats, and blue jeans.

The penitentiary had bought three thousand orange jackets, but inmates saw the jackets as the administration's attempt to embarrass them, so they were not used for fear of creating a riot, and no jeans were allowed on the Hill. We had accepted both inventories to clean up their mess.

I asked if my responses or input would be part of the final audit report. King said yes, if Bob would allow it.

I told King that an audit required input so there would be a complete record. I said that Bob's use of the mismanagement RCW was a flawed theory. To be a crime, Bob would have to show intent, and retroactive budget cuts did not amount to overspending.

King said, "I will pass on your concerns to Director Peterson."

* * *

Lippold accepted the attorney general's decision on the airport/county screening agreement, but he still felt I was wrong.

On Bob's next visit, I offered my resignation. I had no respect for Bob. I wanted his answer immediately; my offer was good for that day only. He said he could not take my letter of resignation.

Weeks later he arrived, smiling, to tell me he would accept it. I kicked him out of my office. Kathy had set the one-day limit—after all, we had five children.

Life remained tough until Bob promoted Dave Savage to be my supervisor. I never again dealt with Lippold. I got on well with Savage, but budget cuts were still budget cuts.

It would be unfair for me to suggest Bob selected me for special treatment; he had similar issues in Vancouver, Washington. In Clark County, Bob even got Amos Reed involved. County commissioners and Reed butted heads, and that WR program closed. Bob had control issues because he held on to his prison-system thinking.

* * *

To make cuts, Kerry Kirking managed two positions. Al Ramos kept custody posts vacant and cut overtime. Gaumer combined some cooks with Spokane Community College's Cooking and Baking School. I used the education program money to which Lippold had previously refused me access. We saved three cook jobs.

With education dollars in play, Gaumer talked to his senior staff about teaching. They turned him down, so he appointed junior staff. Each got a $7 per hour pay raise and fewer hours as instructors because they became SCC employees.

I survived the 1982 budget cuts but the 1983-84 biennium budget gave no relief. Dave was vague about funding and he could not alter reality with kind words.

Amos Reed never visited Geiger nor did he limit cuts. I felt it was unrealistic for staff to run on thin air. It was just a matter of time before we hit a wall with an event or incident.

But Reed had national credentials, a prophetic bearing, and a direct line to Governor Spellman. Complain to Reed and he showed you his frayed drapes and said, "Sacrifice!" He continued to press his agenda even as public support thinned.

Amos was racing time. He appeared regal, gracious, smooth, and patient, but he wanted results or he would erupt.

In spring 1983, Amos arrived at a legislative tour, headed by a Senate committee chair, which toured Geiger. I had not been aware Amos was even in town. The committee flew in on the governor's plane to tour Geiger and look at our toy factory. A ninety-year-old woodworker had provided tools and drawings and trained inmates to start the factory; it offset some of our lost programming by keeping fifteen inmates busy and positive. We had been covered on local TV.

No staff was assigned, as inmates rotated workstations and trained their own replacements. Inmates learned blueprint reading and math. There was no pay, yet inmates lined up to work. We had a waiting list, and those who lacked a high school diploma had to go to school to get on the list. Building toys kept inmates busy, so violation rates dropped.

Just ten workers and five trainees produced three hundred toys a month. The toys were given to hospitals and daycares. Inmates with children were able to send home one toy each month. The Senate committee chair inquired about getting toys for the Tacoma Child Care Hospital, and after the tour our group ate with her at the Longhorn Café.

Amos walked in and sat across from us. The senator talked about toys while Amos told tales and jokes. Up close, Amos had slightly gray, sandy hair. He did not look seventy years old as he warmed up his prey. He had not seen Geiger, but the senator had told him about her visit and the needs at the hospital.

Reed said, "Senator, we will ship you the toys."

I tried to shift the discussion to Reed. He had lived in North Carolina, so I spoke about plantation architecture. Amos mentioned decorative mouse holes.

"You lived in the South," Reed said. "What was the reason for mouse holes? Do you know?"

"No idea," I replied.

Amos laughed. "So folks know where to put traps."

He laughed as he left. He must have gotten his money in the budget.

After lunch the committee went to Pine Lodge. We were late due to Amos, so there was no time for a tour. Staffers were worried the governor's pilot would be upset. The Senate chair said not to worry—Spellman needed her votes and she had gotten her toys. They toured as planned.

Her goodwill gave me hope that Geiger would get a fair chance in hard times.

* * *

I taught a survival class at Geiger in late 1982, which helped me remember why the hassle was worth the effort. My class was ten inmates and met for two hours on Wednesday mornings for six weeks.

The topics discussed were many. We discussed jails, prisons, society, hurtful behavior, inmate power, supervision, work, choices, etc. I cycled the topics and issues.

We talked of arrest, police attitudes, prison frustrations, con code, and street life. I let students push boundaries. I listened and did not push back. I responded openly. The topic was not the point. I wanted dialogue to get inmates thinking.

I worked in a people business, first to protect citizens and next to reform those who had made mistakes. Offenders caught up in anger did not see their bias—blame was easier than accountability.

To reduce tension, I offered compliments here and there. It was a sales ploy to break defenses. It was interesting to watch tough guys get caught up in the ego trap.

Without crooks there would be no police, no prosecutors, no judges, no probation, and no prisons. They were the lifeblood of the system and I wanted them to know that. I hoped to show how their criminal acts created a living for me. Geiger had not existed, but they and others gave up parts of their lives. I discussed the con code and the fear and anger that sustained it, which was a cost to them.

* * *

At Geiger I matured as a leader. I found that it was desirable for staff to have ownership of their mission. I answered questions and set limits. I learned that doubts did not prevent staff from being effective. Honest people sometimes disagreed, so it was okay to question each other.

The Sentencing Reform Act made pre-sentence investigations less useful—the goal was to punish crime, so power shifted from judges to plea-bargaining prosecutors. Supervision lost out, as prisons were more valued than probation and rehabilitation.

I saw that in daily activity we did not treat others as we wished to be treated. Feelings were hurt and denial clouded the judgment of staffers.

As the earthquakes occurred downtown I stayed focused on Geiger, thinking I was off the fault line. I was wrong.

Pine Lodge Corrections Center 1983–1991

Ross Peterson, the director of community corrections, called me in mid-June 1983. I had known Ross as a parole board member and in the WCA. I had not talked to him since Bob Lippold had arrived in the agency. Ross told me to be in his office in Olympia at 10 a.m. on Friday. I figured it was about the budget or Geiger programming. Ross was a Lippold supporter.

When I stepped off the elevator and walked into Peterson's office on Friday, I came face to face with Kip Kautzky, the director of prisons.

Ross was upbeat as he told Kip about my work with the WCA and Geiger. There was no talk of Lippold. "What is going on?" I wondered.

Kip seemed impressed and offered me the superintendent post at Pine Lodge. I did not refuse. Peterson said Peggy Hoffman was going to become the Spokane regional administrator.

Peterson turned to Kip and said, "So be it."

"Kip, thank you for the opportunity," I said.

Ross relaxed. Kip shook my hand, said, "I'll see you downstairs after lunch," and left.

Ross asked me to sit and all of a sudden we were best friends. We did not talk of Geiger—that was history. I would leave Geiger within weeks. That was that.

I was in a new ball game. Ross said Ernie Packebush would go to Geiger to ensure a smooth transition. I smiled—Ernie had already been selected. It was a good thing I did not ask for time to think it over. Ernie had been dropping in routinely for months.

Ross was unaware that Ernie and Ron Myers had had a feud back at the Spokane County Jail in 1971. Ernie and Ron had both graduated from Eastern Washington University, but given their history, a train wreck was in the making. Maybe that was the plan, but I did not need to think about Geiger anymore.

* * *

The Oyster House on Bud Inlet was near headquarters. I had a bowl of chowder and met headquarters staff. They said hello, but none asked me questions. Word of my new position was not yet out.

Until I saw Kip, nothing would be settled. I would have a heart-to-heart with him.

I arrived early and found Kip at his desk in shirtsleeves. He was tall and clean-cut, I guessed in his mid-forties. He looked younger with his full head of dark hair. In Ross's office he had smiled, but now he was sharp.

His first words were, "I hear you're a pain in the ass."

I said, "I'm a bastard if you ignore policies and lie to me."

Kip smiled. "We'll get on fine. I do not lie. I follow my policies and I expect staff to do the same."

I knew I would like Kip.

After our exchange, I saw a shadow off to the side. Deputy Director of Prisons Jim Spalding was at the table. I would report to him.

Kip said, "You have a big job ahead. Pine Lodge is a high-cost unit. With cuts ahead, I doubt you will stay open. Your costs are high, and there are escapes. With mandatory screening, Pine Lodge is never full.

"Welcome aboard," he continued. "You report July 5."

I left Olympia for Sea-Tac Airport near mid-afternoon. I did not call Kathy so she would not worry. Kathy had lived through nine years of Geiger to this point, and she was just glad I had a job and a paycheck.

* * *

On Monday I thanked my staff at Geiger and answered questions to get ahead of the rumors. I stressed the need to start positive with Ernie.

County staffers voiced their concerns, but Geiger had been built on cooperation and I said they must ensure that cooperation continued. I would be down the road just eight miles but it may as well have been a hundred. I would not get involved at Geiger.

Ron Myers spoke to me in private about his conflicts with Ernie. I told Ron to worry about himself before worrying about Ernie. Perhaps Leon Mayer would be a bridge until they found common ground. "You are both adults," I reminded him.

I worried for my staff. It struck me that I had not prepared them for change or told them that change is what you make of it. Still, my staff had done good work and built the program.

On my last day, I offered to help Ernie if he needed it. He thanked me, but I did not seriously await his call; if Lippold had wanted my input, he would not have moved me.

I told Ernie that I would stay out of his business. I said my goodbyes, keeping them brief. When mid-morning coffee and cake were finished, I left Geiger.

Walking out, it struck me that it took five years to open Geiger, and in that time I had essentially owned it. But once Geiger opened I had shared it with others. Putting it in context would take time. Memories were bittersweet, but it was a heck of a run.

* * *

On the day I walked out of Geiger I had a call from Frank, the probationer to whom I had loaned $100 for boots in 1965. I had not seen him since. He had moved to Canada and gone to college. Afterward he became a drug and alcohol counselor, and was now married with children. He asked me if he could risk attending his son's wedding in Yakima, Washington.

I told him, "You'd better check on your warrant status."

Frank stayed in Canada and I wished him well.

* * *

On Tuesday, July 5, 1983, my red 1964 Chevrolet Nova coupe traveled west, past Geiger, to Medical Lake. I was Pine Lodge's third superintendent, and I felt apprehensive. It was a hot day.

I had bought the Nova as a school car for Shawn and Kelly, but neither drove a stick, so I had inherited it. Embarrassed at my old car, I did not use the superintendent's parking slot.

I felt sorry for myself; this was the first day in twenty years that I went to work because of the money. I did not want to work in a prison.

I walked with purpose, stiff-legged, to the front gate. In 1977 I had been on the startup team and the weeds were waist high. Now, the PLCC grounds were manicured lawns under a high canopy of ponderosa pines.

Five staffers greeted me at the gate. Their hello was friendly. On the sidewalk, I passed two inmates headed to Walker Hall.

"Hello, sir," one said.

The other nodded and said, "Mr. Heffernan."

I caught his eye as we passed.

At the main door the locks popped and the door opened into a sally port. A second group of staffers shook my hand. Their greetings seemed to be genuine. I saw faces I recalled from 1978, but I did not remember names.

Gary Jones, the correctional program manager, guided me on a tour. I tried not to be the focus as we moved from the first to the second floor. The dorms and halls shined. I saw eyes peering from dorms as we walked.

In 1976, with Hal Bradley, I had seen Pine Lodge piled with junk and in disrepair. The remodel had done wonders, and the extra-wide halls felt airy. Housing had once been single rooms for female mental patients, but in the remodel living units were converted to open bays.

To the northeast was a fenced recreation yard. Beyond the recreation yard was the Interlake School, a facility for impaired youth, and further north was Eastern State Hospital. A twelve-foot perimeter fence enclosed Pine Lodge's housing.

The total campus was thirty-three acres, with Walker Hall on the fence line and the Lake View Apartments on Medical Lake. The town of Medical Lake sat to the east across blue lake waters.

Pine Lodge was a two-story, red brick building built circa 1930. It had four dorms on the back side of the building, each with a capacity of twenty inmates. The first floor housed the dining hall, administrative offices, medical room, and main control for the front gate.

The wide marble stairs were on the north and south midway down each side of the main hall. The second floor had holding cells just above master control. The west part of the second floor had recreation space and counselors' offices, while the east, once used as a business office, was now a classroom. At both ends of the corridors were large glassed-in porches.

Bay windows stood open to catch the breeze off the lake. The sight of idle inmates surprised me—on a Tuesday morning they should have been working, not sitting.

And more important, escapes were an issue at PLCC, yet there were open windows. Looking at the open windows I wondered, "Why bother to lock the doors?"

* * *

The tour ended in the administrative area in front of my office. The space was dorm-size and mostly vacant. Desks were scattered about. A conference room was connected to the administrative area. I started to say, "I enjoyed my tour," when suddenly I was interrupted.

"There is an escape from Walker Hall!" a staffer said.

At Pine Lodge less than an hour, I had my first escape. That must have been a record. The inmate count confirmed that two inmates were gone.

Because escapes had occurred often, I expected the staff to know the drill. I looked for professionalism, a practiced response that was absent. Instead I saw confusion and panic.

I understood that part of being superintendent was role-playing, so I stayed low key. I stepped back and let events play out. I had to show the staff that I was professional. I wanted them to do their jobs and not worry about me. I had seen escapes and I would see others. Work must go on. For the escapees, it was only a matter of time before they were arrested.

I told the staff that one inmate we had passed earlier had waved good-bye. He had escaped from Geiger once. By midmorning, staffers were still wide eyed. I called off our chase and held a briefing. I used the escape to show the staff that I did not play blame games.

I owned up to the escape. We evaluated and assessed the event to better plan and train for the next escape. It was my opportunity to evolve a better plan.

"Was law enforcement notified?" I asked. "Did we call local press, Olympia, and security at the hospital? Do we have any neighbors we should call? How long is it productive to stay on a high escape response?

"Let's talk about this," I said.

* * *

Walker Hall, the escape site, was a wood frame building with windows outside our fence. It was named for Lieutenant Danny Walker, who had died in an accident responding to an escape. I had once attempted to hire Dan at Geiger.

Escapes were part of our business. With escapes, you cannot say when the next will occur, but you can predict where and how. We studied the landscape to assess likely routes. Pine Lodge had limited vehicle access, so we set up intercept posts at traffic junctions.

I had three lieutenants on staff, so I assigned one to review past escapes to learn how and why inmates ran. We needed to identify the factors at PLCC that caused runners; I felt that fear in the dorms was likely a main reason.

Alone at my desk, I got to work. I called Jim Spalding and told him I held a new one-hour-escape-club record. Jim wanted my assessment.

I told him we had work ahead of us, but that the escape would give me cause to move forward rapidly.

Pine Lodge was a top-down unit—Peggy had involved herself in every aspect of daily life, causing staff to look first to her when, perhaps, they should have acted themselves.

The escape was my opportunity to see staff under stress and observe their reactions. Some accepted the facts and moved on while others, caught in the moment, could not. But after that day, no one would argue about creating a valid escape plan.

At shift change I focused on the positives. I told arriving staff that the needed calls had been made. I assured them that we would learn. One escapee had run from Geiger. He had soon been arrested and sent to the penitentiary.

He had had two bites at the apple, but the clock was ticking. It was only a matter of time before an arrest. I took questions from the oncoming shift and we talked about budget and headquarters concerns.

We had to cut our budget. Our daily costs were too high. I spoke of the budget so staff would have a bit more to talk about later. They passed my comments on to the graveyard shift, who passed them on to the day shift.

I told them that if we did not change our image we would be a target for closure. I wanted staff input, both negative and positive. I stressed the importance of dialogue. From that point on, staff input shaped programs.

At 5 p.m. I left. I had earned my wages. I spent no time thinking about Geiger. On the drive home I reviewed items that needed attention at PLCC.

* * *

The business office had two accountants and a business manager, Mike McInnis. On my second day at PLCC, I visited the business office at Lake View and found out that Mike was to go on reserve duty with the National Guard for forty-five days. Before he left, the state auditor, on his standard five-year cycle, issued an audit for PLCC. The state auditor found that a staff member had signed for a

July 1 delivery as if it had been delivered on June 29, in the prior biennium. This falsification of a document caused staff to run for cover and took the wind out of resistance to my requests.

Business operations were the lone area where Peggy had delegated her authority; Mike had been able to stop purchases to ask for more data and controlled operations by denying or delaying purchases. I would not support such veto power.

I visited Lake View daily to review prior budgets, learning the PLCC budget cycle down to the subcategory level. I looked for soft spots. A budget is like a ship on water—you can try to slow it down, but it is always in motion. Budgets do not turn on a dime.

At Geiger I had learned that valid data was vital to staying on course with a spending plan. State agencies used a central accounting system called AFRIS to track spending against allotments. The Office of Financial Management produced reports for agencies that divided data into categories and sub-functions. The reports arrived at PLCC after a three-month journey.

I required data access in real-time, but at PLCC I got resistance when I asked to see numbers, as Mike held his budget close. Old habits died hard. But I needed information—money affected my decisions.

My request was difficult for accountant Anne Schemer, who worked for Mike.

"I'm the boss," I told her. "What I ask for I get, Mike or no Mike."

Mike played catch-up once he returned from reserve duty. My changes upset him at times, and he resisted because of standard management practices at other prisons. He batched purchases to slow walk orders. I reviewed my requests with him, asking what part he did not understand. Eventually Mike complied and the data flowed.

Later, Anne discovered that she had added a zero to a line item in the budget, so that the $100,000 read $1,000,000. I reported this to Jim Spalding, who said to hold money in reserve.

* * *

In the days ahead, I listened to my staff so I could build on their strengths and not tear them down. Gary Jones, the corrections program manager, was a good man, yet forceful and difficult. He was a hardnosed redhead who worked hard. Gary had hired on at the WSP and was later promoted into Pine Lodge. He also had liked Peggy Hoffman as superintendent.

Peggy Hoffman had called to offer help after the escape attempt on my first day. I thanked her and told her I would call if I had questions. I asked her for advice, though she disagreed with many of my changes. Peggy had invested a lot in PLCC. Peggy had had a quiet but firm presence in operations up to and including inmate discipline because she felt it was essential to rehabilitation.

Unlike Peggy, I delegated tasks and authority and asked Gary to do likewise. For Gary, an ex-marine, my request was difficult.

During my first week, it became clear that Gary supported staffers who followed orders. He was uncertain about those who questioned him or had doubts. Gary was a command and control type of manager. His response to me was "Yes, sir; how high, sir?"

Gary guaranteed that staffers would welcome my leadership, but I doubted if he would welcome me over time.

My discipline style was simple, swift, and certain, so inmates saw the results. In disciplinary hearings, if a staffer had followed DOC policy, their decision was final. I acted only if a staffer failed to follow policy. Staffers had to feel that I was aware of both their successes and failures, but that would not work if no one questioned me.

After three or four hearings, my message was clear: follow policy and use common sense. Gary likely disagreed, but he said nothing.

My style made some staff uncomfortable. Staffers were uneasy as I accepted results without comment. I asked my staff, "Why should inmate mistakes consume our time?" I preferred that staff spend time helping inmates achieve program goals.

I was not a prison person or a controlling leader. I wanted the respect of both staff and inmates. To gain their respect, I listened and asked questions. I wanted my staff to empower inmates with options and choices.

Gary filled my leadership vacuum and neutralized my style; while I sought staff input, Gary gave instructions, and it became an issue. However, he was loyal and he did not ask others to do more than he did.

After some run-ins, I expected him to push back. But I had misjudged Gary—I continued to get softball questions. Gary skirted issues as I empowered staff.

* * *

My ability to delegate grew after a bomb threat in August 1983. The call came to our control room at 6 p.m.: "A bomb goes off at midnight." I was at home, but returned immediately.

On my drive, thoughts flew about as I figured out what to do. Gary Jones was gone—Sergeant Ronald Smith was on duty. When I arrived he gave me a clear briefing with options and his plan.

He wanted to call in an air force bomb-sniffing dog at 10 p.m. to screen housing. He would move inmates to the big yard before the dog arrived and call in law enforcement to guard the yard. He had already talked to Olympia's officer of the day.

Smith was matter-of-fact in implementing his plan. I suggested just one improvement. We did not know how inmates would react to a yard ringed with police and guns.

If things went badly the inmates would want to talk to me, so it would be best if I was not there. Smith could say he would check with me as a passive response. I left Pine Lodge at 9:30 and sat on a nearby hill.

It crossed my mind that my location might be hard to explain if a bomb went off. Yet Smith had a plan. Events unfolded as Smith expected—no bomb. At 1 a.m., with the inmates back in dorms, I headed home.

I saw Smith the next day and thanked him for the staff's effort. He was happy that I had let him handle the event. He had expected

I would take over in front of his staff, as if he did not know what to do. Instead, staffers had seen that I trusted him.

* * *

PLCC staffers had heard that I was hardnosed with Geiger cuts. Staff members expected strong reactions, so they were caught off guard.

Labor contracts called for staff input on work conditions. Gary struggled due to his military life, college, and time at the penitentiary. He made it difficult for a dialogue so I relied on union shop stewards for input and support.

I suggested eliminating prescreening to keep beds full. Staff supported that action.

I had decided to make PLCC a work camp the day I arrived. Pine Lodge had opened as a medium-security institution, and staffing levels were set by that classification level. In 1979 Pine Lodge had been reduced to a minimum-custody facility. Within the prison division, a minimum facility staff had a lieutenant and five sergeants, so we needed to make cuts. I eliminated two of the three lieutenant slots and one sergeant position. Two lieutenants retired voluntarily. The Washington Public Employees Union accepted the changes, as lieutenants were not union staff.

I expected resistance from staff on the next major issue. I wanted to change custody staffers' work weeks from four ten-hour shifts to five eight-and-a-half-hour shifts. The union opposed that move; they liked four-day work weeks with three days off.

They had their say and time passed. I explained that maintaining the current shifts could cause us to be closed. We were the only ten-hour-shift institution, and our per-bed costs were 20 percent above other prisons'. Our costs were the highest in the state, and with escapes added to it, locals would not accept Pine Lodge expansion.

We talked and talked and I listened before making the work schedule change. We cut the number of posts and overtime costs to come in line with other institutions. Security staffers used strong words, yet I still attended their union Christmas party.

A second more positive result of the shift realignment was it allowed us to move vacant custody slots to kitchen, maintenance, and medical facilities. We had previously had staffers who were untrained and not paid properly, and it was not fair to require that. Now we took steps to ensure that staff who were assigned jobs had the training and the skill to do their work.

All my changes upset some staff, including two sergeants seeking to promote to lieutenant. Both transferred, creating vacancies.

I filled one sergeant position to oversee work crews. Promotion was based solely on oral board performance. I promoted whoever had the highest score—in this case it was Dave Perry. Dave was shocked, as he was a union man, a Medical Lake town boy, and a vocal rebel. By promoting Dave, I earned union support.

Work crew slots were plum jobs. Their work shift was from eight to five, Monday until Friday, with holidays off, and they were able to work offsite. Inmates liked working in the community, and Dave's effort and connections expanded our crew work into city parks and onto hospital grounds.

When Perry later expanded offsite job crews, we assigned a second staffer to monitor work sites. He made contacts with new job supervisors to ensure we met their needs.

We offered supervised crews and paid staff costs. The agencies supplied the tools, materials, and a project manager to ensure quality. Agencies paid inmates a dollar per hour. Ten-man crews cost just ten dollars per hour, so crews were always busy with various projects. I made weekly visits to the chow hall and talked to inmates. I got a sense of their mood and asked about the food. Work crews were always upbeat.

* * *

Changes to daily operations were made possible by an escape study. One flaw in the 1978 PLCC remodel was that the doors locked, but the windows did not. Inmates built screens for the windows in a welding class. Spokane Community College staff tested and awarded welding certificates.

The screens were not to penitentiary standards, but inmates would have to work, not merely jump out. We stopped impulsive escapes.

With windows screened, I removed the perimeter posts and guns. The guns were transferred to the penitentiary. This eliminated firearms training, dusk-to-dawn postings, and the armory sergeant. We saved $200,000, but my decision ensured Pine Lodge would stay a minimum facility, which meant it would be harder to avoid closure.

Change was hard and staffers complained. Yet I no longer had to worry that staff may shoot a nineteen-year-old inmate off our fence or, worse, hit a patient or citizen.

* * *

The escape assessment took months. The analysis showed that inmate-on-inmate acts such as violence prompted escapes. In my first three months there were nine assaults due to idleness and bullying. I installed a no-tolerance policy. If an inmate caused a fight, or made a threat, we shipped him out.

Only half the inmates had jobs. The others slept all day and raised hell all night. I wanted inmates to be busy all day so the dorms would be quiet. I wanted each inmate to have a job that required eight hours of work, five days a week.

Pine Lodge needed painting, so we created paint crews overseen by experienced staff members. Crews washed walls, scraped them, and applied two coats of paint. All unassigned inmates worked, and they painted every surface at Pine Lodge.

The paint crews had a motto: if it is not moving, paint it. The project lasted four months, which gave us time to create other jobs. We had the floors cleaned to a shine so it would be clear that staff were in control. We stopped screening inmates and took whoever was referred to us, but inmates off the chain bus immediately saw that staff ran Pine Lodge, not the inmates.

I took advantage of the painting to move my office into Walker Hall and move the business office next door. Gary Jones moved into my old office and now had more autonomy. We also divided the administration space into a classroom and clerical offices. The space on PLCC's top floor opened for a fifth dorm.

The old business office at Lake View became the upholstery school and shop. Skilled students ran the cottage industry, which cut overhead costs.

GED school became mandatory for those with no diploma, and all unassigned inmates went to school.

Janet Anderson, a bilingual teacher at Community Colleges of Spokane, began using inmates to tutor other inmates who were non-English speakers. We printed our rules in Spanish, and Janet had volunteers work one-on-one with Spanish-speaking inmates. She graduated ten inmates a month with diplomas or GEDs. We later moved her to Walker Hall, so working inmates could attend night school. An education was what inmates took with them when they left PLCC.

* * *

The prior therapeutic model had not been well defined. Inmates often had many infractions before transfer from PLCC. The old model suggested that mistakes were expected, so tolerance was high. PLCC staff had bought into that old model, so there were struggles as I shifted to a no-nonsense approach.

I had no tolerance for manipulators, as they did not fit in an environment where choices were allowed and important. I wanted each inmate to be safe and fear free so the worst 10 percent would not consume our time.

It was six months before staff saw merit in the inmate self-screening policy. We accepted everyone except high-profile inmates or those with escape histories. Those were simply too risky.

Within two months, assaults dropped to one a month, then one every six months as inmates learned our limits. They did not want to risk transfer after seeing others ride out on chain buses. Living conditions improved for inmates and life got easier for staff as inmates accepted the rules.

Yet nothing is easy even when a line is drawn. One of the inmates working on the painting project, Michael, was the first out of bed, the last to quit, and worked hard all day. He liked to paint and did well. His talent and work ethic set a high standard that annoyed lazy workers. Dissension grew.

One young inmate baited Michael, calling him a nigger. No staffers heard the offensive word. Finally Michael exploded, saying, "If you don't shut your mouth, I'll kick your ass." Staffers did hear that. Michael was found guilty of threatening and a transfer loomed.

Michael asked for an exception due to the quality of his work and the fact that the word nigger was not right. I did not agree. Our rule stood—he could return in ninety days.

"I'll not return," he said. "I've earned the right to stay."

If I allowed him to stay it would send a mixed message.

"Have a good day," I told him. "Threats aren't okay."

He left mad. I did not see Michael again until he walked off a chain bus back at PLCC. He was going to work release in Seattle. After spending time at the penitentiary Michael appreciated our fear-free prison. We extended extra help and found him work with a paint contractor in Seattle. Michael left PLCC for Seattle after sixty days, all smiles.

* * *

Gary Jones hired Willie Wilson in 1984 to oversee our kitchen as food service manager. He saved us money and improved the food. PLCC had been paying for two meals a day from the Eastern State Hospital campus kitchen since startup in 1978. It cost $4 per meal, and staffers transported the food from the campus kitchen in hot carts, so meals arrived either overdone or cold. Food ended up in garbage cans, which doubled costs. With Willie, I set a goal to cut costs by 50 percent and create inmate jobs. Wilson did a meal survey and cooked meals the inmates actually ate.

The medical area also needed converting. A doctor came in weekly for sick call; any daily sick calls required moving inmates to the ESH campus doctor. We opened a job position for a nurse as support. With a nurse running the daily sick call and pill line, we cut costs and provided better care.

We hired a new maintenance supervisor to cut dependence on ESH maintenance staff. We used skilled inmate journeymen for projects and stayed within union guidelines for on-campus trades.

It would be misleading to say we grew in an orderly way. That was not the case—growth occurred non-sequentially, with starts, spurts, and confusion. Yet we slowly drove Pine Lodge's population up and our costs down.

What was stable was our commitment to inmate safety and PLCC's mission. As safety improved our escapes dropped. By providing school options, we gave inmates a chance to learn to work, read, and write. We stuck to these basics so as not to confuse inmates or ourselves.

* * *

My contacts with Jim Spalding were crisp and distant. Doug Jacques, his liaison, visited every other week to observe and learn our agenda. Doug likely saw more changes than he liked, but he did not rein me in or slow me down.

I had not known Spalding when I was in Walla Walla. He had been promoted to the reformatory as a lieutenant and then a captain under Roger Maxwell.

Monroe Superintendent Dale Swenson had sent Jim to college so he would be qualified to be promoted to an associate superintendent at Washington State Reformatory. Spalding spoke highly of Swenson and his time at Monroe.

Doug Vinzant had been fired in 1978, and Jim became superintendent at the penitentiary and put the prison on lockdown. He later moved on to Olympia as assistant director in the prison division.

My ongoing visits with Jim were brief but friendly. Jim's concern was the penitentiary, and he was wary of me. We did not connect socially. Jim was an angler, low-key and easygoing. He considered Pine Lodge to be my job, and expected me to handle it. He did not mix in my business, and had let me settle in at Pine Lodge as issues of closure continued.

* * *

In 1984, Medical Lake City Manager Tom Bumgardner asked if a school track team could use our shoreline for cross-country racing. I checked with Eastern State Hospital Superintendent Dr. Ulysses Watson. He said yes, as long as runners stayed on the shoreline. The school races were a success and Bumgardner asked the DSHS for a shoreline trail.

The DSHS and the city council approved the trail. The council wanted federal funds to pay for construction from the community development fund.

Also in 1984, Lieutenant Tim Delp was promoted to McNeil Island, and Lieutenant Al Ramos transferred from Geiger to PLCC as his replacement. Al and I got on well, but still I asked Al to honor the chain of command and report to Gary so no issues would develop. Gary and Al seemed to work well together even though Al had not been Gary's first choice.

Al Ramos worked with the Department of Natural Resources (DNR) as they moved into the Lake View Apartments. The DNR held firefighting contracts with state and national forests and had contracted with the Department of Corrections to use inmates on fire crews. The DNR provided supervision and training, and we provided custody and inmates. The DNR brought in trucks, equipment, and operating dollars. The fire camp helped us because we needed more jobs as our population grew.

With the DNR we had a new voice opposing Pine Lodge's closure, talk of which persisted because of our high bed costs.

We had no capital funds nor did I expect any. My requests were denied. My solution was to increase bed count within our existing site footprint and budget.

We reconfigured the dorms to gain eight beds per dorm and improved privacy with dividers paid for and built by SCC classes. Our count grew to 125, which cut per-bed costs from $61 to $40 per day.

I was required to submit yearly organization charts for review. We had shifted staff positions in 1984, so I was not surprised when

Kip Kautzky called to talk about our staffing assignment chart. Gary Jones joined me to help answer Kip's questions.

We entered Kip's fifth-floor office in Olympia and were told that our chart was weak on custody and needed to align with prison standards.

"What is he thinking?" I wondered. I did not see Kip's point about understaffing. We returned to our chart confused and without specific details. A second try got the same result: "Review your chart."

Gary studied charts from another camp and found they had added a captain position. Gary currently supervised both our unit teams and custody.

Adding a new manager made no sense, as Gary was not overworked. Yet Kip was serious, and Gary argued to add a captain or we would have to stay in Olympia.

"What will a captain do?" I asked.

We brainstormed duties such as overseeing work crews, writing policy, transportation, food service, graveyard shift, and liaison to the DNR or police. We returned to Kip's office, but before we entered I stopped Gary and asked if he could accept these changes.

Gary said, "Submit it."

Kip accepted our submission. Gary would have to adjust or I would have a mess. We had a quiet flight back to Spokane.

* * *

Al Ramos was my choice for captain. Al had been working for Gary and I had heard no complaints. In my mind Al was the frontrunner, but the selection process required us to interview five candidates.

Jim Spalding chaired the panel, which also included myself and Jim Geiger from Larch Mountain, a DNR fire camp near Vancouver, Washington. In a pre-panel meeting I learned that Spalding and Al had a history. At the WSP, Al had led a walkout over safety issues. Jim had not forgotten; he preferred two other candidates for captain.

Interviews took all day; Al was the best and Spalding agreed to his appointment. Al increased the number of work crews and strengthened both security and policies. Yet Al and Gary clashed.

Both were headstrong, type-A personalities and they had issues dating back to the WSP. Either one could be a troublemaker on a given day. At first I ignored them, but that proved to be a bad choice, as their conflict created confusion and inhibited teamwork.

The staff split into camps, and the stress became a distraction. I saw no retreat. It was a puzzle I could not solve. I thought, "I must be the hammer." But I was not a hammer. We stayed afloat only because Lieutenant Harold Hays remained above the conflict.

Finally I insisted that the conflicts end.

"Your conflicts have become a Pine Lodge issue," I told Gary and Al. "Handle it or I will fire you both."

The surface friction stopped, but it was not a happy time. It was a long year, but we passed audits, cut costs, and increased the inmate population. I refused to take sides. The ebb and flow was ongoing. Kelly's Rule compounds Murphy's Law, stating, "If it can go wrong, it will at the worst possible time."

* * *

The first escape had allowed me to push change for a year. Yet all things slow in time, so I needed a new spark.

I took an idea from the five-year plan for Spokane's Expo '74. Looking at items five years away was not as threatening as immediate issues, but it was close enough to set goals.

When I spoke of a five-year plan I heard no cautions, so I submitted an outline, which Doug Jacques took to Jim Spalding. If Jim asked questions it would be his way of saying no. Spalding was focused on operations and budget, not our five-year plan, so I heard nothing from Jim, but Kautzky called to say he liked the draft and wanted updates after I completed a staff survey.

It took six months to complete my second, more complete draft.

I collected staff input and expectations of PLCC programs, organizations, services, and facilities. Managers were the first to give their input in one-hour visits, as I felt they needed to know what I was asking staff, though staff input was confidential.

I did not want rumors to start among the staff. My focus was what was best for Pine Lodge. I asked, "What needs fixing? What changes should we make? What keeps you motivated?"

I finished in mid-February 1985. My draft had an introduction, a statement of objectives and goals, and a twenty-page, double-spaced summary. Management had ranked suggestions based on complexity and resources.

I sent the draft to Kip for review. He wrote comments and returned the plan. I rewrote it and sent it back. Kip called to say he liked it but could not okay it because his division lacked a comparable plan. We were way out in front, but his next budget would list bullet issues that tied costs to solutions as in our plan.

We introduced the five-year plan locally as our roadmap. I did yearly interviews with staff. No report went to Olympia, but the results became our report card for the prior year, allowing staff to adjust goals annually. Staffers saw their input creating results.

I wanted Olympia's attention so they would invest in PLCC's survival.

* * *

The DNR's fire crews were needed in the Spokane fire belt. Eric Martenson was the first DNR superintendent. He stood six feet six inches tall, so we were a sight tramping about together, a real Mutt and Jeff team. Once, on a walk with Eric, I complained that headquarters did not see our potential because we were not visible.

The next Monday, trucks, a bulldozer, and a road grader arrived at PLCC from the DNR.

"What do you want done?" the crew asked me. "We're on fire training."

Dirt was moved, hills leveled, valleys filled. "Fire training" ended and there were five acres of flat land east of our fence, graded and with staked elevations.

I thanked them, the equipment rolled back on trailers, and the convoy left. I never saw a bill.

Visitors saw the flat land beyond the fence. Rumors flew when Doug or Jim visited; neither could believe the DNR had done the work.

Jim Spalding endorsed a plan to have a home builders class construct a supply building and a new upholstery shop. Headquarters also paid to replace PLCC's roof for $250,000. We were finally part of the budgetary agenda.

The DNR acquired land west of Pine Lodge and erected a shop, and later built a regional office there. Our best upholstery students worked for the DNR making fire packs designed by a DNR staff member and being sold in western states.

The PLCC construction moved forward with no site plan. We built as we were able. Citizens and local politicians said we were good neighbors. Escapes remained in single digits, which gave us freedom to grow our inmate population.

Mostly good things happened after the DNR arrived, with one exception.

Four inmates on a DNR thinning crew drank beer purchased by one of the inmates in Deer Park, Washington. They felt uneasy as their bus started for Pine Lodge, as they knew the PLCC staff would smell the beer. At the intersection of Maple Street and Third Avenue in Spokane, the four inmates took over the bus in rush hour traffic.

The DNR supervisor and six inmates who were not involved jumped off and ran to a café to call PLCC. The inmates on the bus did not know they were near I-90, just eighteen miles from Idaho. The inmate driving turned against one-way traffic and the inmates abandoned the bus. Police with guns in hand chased and captured the escapees. I felt lucky that no one had been shot.

To my knowledge, no crew had ever taken over a DNR bus. Most inmates respected their chance to work, which is why the six inmates had jumped off with the staffer.

* * *

In midsummer 1985, I got a call one night from my sister-in-law. My brother, Jim, had been in an accident. He had driven off a back road in Stevens County, hurtled down a hillside, and hit a car that was up on jacks. Two people had died; another was in serious condition.

Jim had been scouting hunting sites and drinking. After he was released from the hospital he was taken to Stevens County Jail on charges of negligent homicide.

My sister-in-law said that Dad was on his way to post bail. Jim needed an attorney—it was serious. I told her I supported Jim, but I could not contact the police and court officials I knew in Stevens County.

Once Jim was bailed out, we visited. He looked bad, but there was nothing we could do. He admitted to drinking. Two people were dead and one was still badly hurt.

He only had minor injuries. I looked into Jim's eyes and saw he would have traded places with the dead, but that was not an option. He talked to an attorney and decided to plead guilty. Dad felt helpless.

Dad and I were in court at Jim's sentencing. He received a prison term of eighteen months, the standard from the SRA grid. Jim turned himself in during November 1985. His insurance paid all medical and other bills, and Jim paid a lump sum to the survivor.

Jim entered prison expecting that inmates would associate him with me. I called Spalding about Jim's arrest as Jim was moved to the reception center. Spalding sent Jim to Cedar Creek Corrections Center.

I talked to Jim by phone every other week, but I did not visit. I told him to stay busy. Work was Jim's legal escape. I did not ask him about his activities or life at Cedar Creek. In December 1986 Jim was transferred to Geiger. Once on WR, we visited at his home.

I did not talk to Jim about Cedar Creek; I knew that many things affect inmates in prison. There is constant fear beyond staffers' views. There is anger and frustration. There is boredom endured as the clock clicks slowly.

Dad entered the hospital in December 1986 with cancer. He had kept his illness quiet as the cancer advanced. I visited Dad before he died peacefully in his sleep, with family around him, on December

26, 1986. It had been seventeen years since my mother's death, yet at that moment it felt like yesterday.

Jim was paroled in mid-1987.

* * *

Sentencing reform continued from 1984 to 1987 as the Department of Corrections built prisons and offered no alternatives. There was a strong political shift toward harsher punishment because citizens saw punishment as a crime stopper. That idea was wrong, yet it consumed money and resources that could have been better spent in communities.

Society supported prisons and decried the use of probation. Prison staff believed that field staffers were elitists. Initially the prison population dropped after the SRA, providing time to build and control prisons. Prisons became big business with probation's death.

People blamed racism for the disproportionate number of blacks in prison, but in fact it was social conditions in families, schools, and lack of opportunity that was causing the lopsided numbers.

* * *

Amos Reed, who had made the DSHS go away in 1981, retired in 1986. At his retirement party, I recalled that I had spoken with Reed only three times. At his retirement I shook his hand. He seemed not to have aged. He had set DOC straight and knocked out DSHS. He left us with prisons and no excuses, and wished us well.

Governor Booth Gardner hired Chase Riveland to head the Department of Corrections as secretary. Chase was a prison man from Colorado who had previously worked in Wisconsin probation and parole. Chase had been at the National Institute of Corrections and studied at the Wharton School of Business. He was also active in the National Correctional Association.

Riveland brought in Nancy Campbell from Colorado as his community corrections director. Her leadership was harsh. A type-A leader, she stirred things up, saying field staff had wobbled off course. I heard ill words, but her goals and priorities were not up for debate.

Campbell's hiring had no immediate effect on me. We heard she lacked a heart and shook things up, pushing female upward mobility. SRA was a sidebar now; it was her way or nothing. Old timers fled or wished they had.

Kip Kautzky had applied for Amos Reed's job but resigned after Chase's appointment and moved to Colorado. Joe Lehman became director of prisons, with Spalding as deputy director. Jim and Joe emphasized staff analysis, post orders, and audits. Joe's energy kept us busy.

I learned that Spalding had major issues with Kip over a meat theft at Monroe in 1982. Jim felt a friend, who resigned over the incident, had been held wrongly accountable. I had not been aware of his feelings.

Chase seemed to like a degree of tension in upper management. Unlike Amos, Chase was no crusader. He handled trouble as it surfaced—he did not search for issues. His governor set his agenda, and the SRA was not on Governor Gardner's radar.

Riveland stayed out of the fray and defended his boss. At a leadership conference shortly after he arrived, Chase said, "My boss's non-issues are my non-issues. Bring me problems and you're a problem."

Chase visited PLCC in the fall 1986. The trip was to see his empire, to get a lay of the land. He had a light tan sport jacket slung over his shoulder and his tie was loose. He was just one of the boys. Chase was wiry and projected energy, yet seemed relaxed. I was impressed. He had a bottom-up managing style that relied on asking and taking questions. Chase listened and was open to new ideas.

I liked what he said; Chase felt like a kindred spirit.

Later I found I had misjudged him. When I thought he was listening, he was observing. He blocked out issues. Chase was a mover and a shaker and not easy to pin down.

Chase did his governor's bidding and did not express his own philosophy. Legal or moral topics were slippery slopes; he would rather just do his job.

Amos had ignored the SRA, leaving staff members poorly trained. Chase implemented reforms in community corrections. He wanted a field team Campbell would like, so he purged the roots of probation. Ross Peterson, Judy Smith, and Robert Lippold were all dismissed.

Peggy Hoffman, the northeast regional administrator, was also caught in the change. Her highest civil service rating was correction program manager (CPM). The only CPM slot in eastern Washington was at PLCC, which she took because she was forced to revert to her civil service level.

Gary Jones transferred to the WSP to open a slot for Peggy at Pine Lodge. Gary was loyal because Peggy had hired him. Few others would have offered up their jobs.

If Peggy had had her choice she would not have returned, but she had no options. We talked about how what she left in 1983 had vanished. She had to accept the work camp model. I did not give her a script, as that was not my style. Peggy carried out our mission with no push back. Her arrival did have the benefit of ending the conflict between Gary and Al. Peggy and Al worked together, productivity improved, and Pine Lodge was a better place to work.

To soften her return, I gave her flextime so she could work on a master's degree at Eastern Washington University. She finished her degree in record time and created programs for sex offenders and for married inmates returning to families. In both groups, she sought new ways of addressing old problems.

Historically, sex offenders in prison hid, denying their offenses to survive, so there was no treatment in prison. Peggy hired professionals to monitor the groups, where members reviewed their past behavior.

The objective for sex offenders was for them to select treatment upon release. If they entered treatment, we considered it a success. Therapy facilitators reinforced their treatment commitment upon release.

Family awareness groups helped offenders reintegrate with families who had lived without them. Their wives had paid bills and made decisions, and their children sat where they had sat. It took time for families to adjust to their return.

Peggy was promoted to a therapist position in the DSHS. Bob Enright assumed her duties and fit right in. He and Al Ramos had been effective at Geiger, and with Bob's knowledge of classification he was a great addition at PLCC.

* * *

Joe Lehman was a whiz on budgets, audits, and politics. Joe brought energy and limited Chase's impact on prisons. Specific prison changes could be a hard sell but Joe designed the changes and implemented them.

Joe liked statistics and long meetings. He talked with energy but was weak on follow up. He rarely provided closure, but with Joe things were never dull—there were new ideas every minute. Staff questioned Joe's quick movement, but his strong legislative contacts made him a good front man.

Historically, prisons were islands against change. Joe networked those islands by way of central classification, taking classification duties away from individual institutions and placing that power in Olympia.

In mid-1987, Joe Lehman asked me to cover Jim Spalding's desk while Jim visited Europe for three weeks. Joe liked managers to taste Olympia as part of staff development.

Kathy, the kids, and I lived at the Greenwood Motor Inn. Kathy had a vacation of sorts and the kids got to see Olympia. We had a poolside room so the children played in the wading pool.

The duty, however, was dull. On my first day I watched boats on Bud Inlet. I had neither authority nor a clue. I started at 8:30 a.m. as superintendents called in reports made by their duty officers. The calls lasted until eleven. I did not tell my peers how to run their prisons. After eleven the phones died. I did nothing but look out the window.

I called Pine Lodge daily, my sole break except for the times Joe looked in and asked, "How are you doing?"

When Joe popped in on the third day, I asked him if I could be more useful. He looked let down but returned with a box of papers.

"Review this," he said. "We'll talk tomorrow."

In that box was a failed attempt to redo RCW Chapter 72, the law that had created the Department of Corrections in 1981. The box was a mess.

"Can I toss this and start over?" I asked. He said yes.

Jim's secretary, Nancy, frowned as I handed her the RCW and asked her to enter it in her computer. She had planned to do some filing. Luckily she had a copy of the RCW on floppy disk and installed it so I could just modify the file. Then she was in a better mood.

I interviewed Joe about the RCW. With his approval I got access to the attorney general.

With my experience drafting House Bill 77 I finished the first draft in three days. Nancy did a copy edit and cleaned it up. My draft went to the attorney general, then Joe and the command managers who headed the three groups of institutions. Chase Riveland saw it last. The title of the bill was "Omnibus Departmental Legislation." It went to the code office as a DOC request in January 1988.

I found that other staff had written bills. One bill was for new hearing rules for SRA violators and staff liability. The focus was post-release monitoring—no one had any interest in engaging offenders in life change. The SRA was a piecemeal system that ignored justice: police arrested but did not charge, prosecutors charged but did not convict, courts convicted but did not set the terms of sentencing.

I returned to Spokane knowing it was a better place than Olympia. My visit had exposed the gap between planning and doing fieldwork, and showed me the tension between concept and practice.

* * *

At Geiger I had met regularly with inmates in an effort to focus our programs and staff. When I brought such sessions to Pine Lodge I faced resistance. Knowledge is power in a prison, so staffers were uneasy about my direct contact with inmates. I stopped my meetings with the condition that unit teams had weekly dialogues.

I walked PLCC's campus daily to get a sense of the mood. After 1986, I started having exit talks with outbound offenders. I wanted their suggestions for improvements or changes.

One of my questions was, "During your prison stay has anyone thanked you for being a prisoner?"

Most often, I saw a double take or a wry smile.

I pointed out, "You make work for police, prosecutors, the courts, and me."

Sometimes a light popped on and an inmate said, "Yeah, I see what you mean. I'm a meal ticket. I won't give you any more work."

That worked for me. Inmates needed to understand that I benefited from their stupidity. That is why I thanked them. Exit talks also satisfied my need for customer input, which I later summarized for the staff.

In my first exit interviews, the worst thing inmates reported was staff. Inmates' lives changed when the shift changed. Inconsistent staff attitudes made life difficult for inmates.

Staffers often denied issues with themselves, but saw ways others could improve. I took no action beyond passing on information, yet in time the best thing inmates reported about Pine Lodge was its staff.

* * *

By 1986, with the SRA in full effect, prisons still needed beds. Amos Reed had created a safety valve in Spokane. He provided funds for a sixth floor of the Spokane County Jail to get locals to vote yes on his capital construction project. The DOC would have access to the new beds if they needed them.

The DOC did need the beds in 1986, so they contracted for forty-six beds in the jail. I was not involved in planning, but did help coordinate jail use and inmate counseling.

If I had planned how the jail would be used, it would have served as a reception unit for felons entering the DOC, because the reception center was across the state in Shelton. But the question was not asked. Instead inmates who had earned minimum custody found themselves in maximum custody.

Tanya Marlton, PLCC liaison, had worked in the jail and at Geiger, so she knew the staff and administrators. She had common sense and was a hard worker.

Jail beds were filled with inmates going to work release. Tanya's job was to ensure a brief stay for the inmates, who felt that their new lodgings were punishment for past good behavior. She quickly moved inmates to Pine Lodge or work release.

Tanya did not stick to old processes—she used her contacts to create a flow. The rotation picked up, so we had no major problems in her unit.

* * *

The Geiger site had its problems, with few shared goals among staff. So county administrators looked to the Federal Bureau of Prisons for contract money. The feds paid twice the state's bed rate and had white-collar criminals. Geiger's contract was up for renewal in 1989 and a train wreck loomed for staff if the contract vanished—without a building to work from, staffers would have no jobs.

Eastern Washington Pre-Release (EWPR) staff started looking for a home. State staff liked the upcoming split, but finding a new site would be difficult because of city and county zoning laws. A new work release unit had opened near the courthouse on Dean Street in Spokane.

I was five years removed from my first tour of Geiger. I had experienced a locating effort for a facility in Spokane. I knew it would not be easy. I believed that EWPR staff would lose their jobs without a site.

I met county officials and asked them to slow down and give time for EWPR to find a facility. Lee Fish, corrections director, agreed but said time was limited.

A delay in place, I met with Regional Administrator Rose Mary Alme. We had lunch and talked about Medical Lake. I told her that Eastern State Hospital was facing cuts, so the community of Medical Lake might accept the pre-release program. Medical Lake was an institution town and liked campus jobs.

I felt that citizens would support EWPR if she talked to the DSHS, who in turn offered vacant units at the Lakeland Village Apartments as a temporary site. The state and county divorced operations at Geiger, but no staff member lost a job. Only diversion suffered as more locals now went to prison.

* * *

Rumors said that EWPR would move to Pine Street across from Pine Lodge. People in Medical Lake liked the idea. It also fit Riveland's logic: why have two facilities when one unit would cost less? Chase was clear that the co-located facilities would be under one superintendent.

I was not part of the EWPR planning. Foundations were installed to the west and south of Pine Lodge for prefabricated modular buildings: the kitchen, housing units, education and recreation spaces, and administration units. The only stick-built structure was a maintenance supply building.

EWPR doubled our site's footprint and population. We added a sixth dorm and a mudroom and grew to 180 beds. Combined with pre-release, the population on the site totaled 350 inmates.

* * *

I was named to a minimum-security prototype task force in 1988. Two camp superintendents, an architect, and an Olympia staffer were also on the task force. Our job was to design a prototype minimum-security unit. Most prison beds were medium-security and we were looking for new options.

We met at North Bend at a state fire-training center. North Bend was the preferred site for the first minimum-security facility, but local citizens objected. We moved our meeting to Olympia where we designed the prototype unit and started a statewide site search.

Olympia officials selected Spokane for the minimum-security camp after the pre-release consolidation at Pine Lodge. Kincheloe had supported the co-location even with all the short-term dilemmas of combining two staffs. My sense was the DOC's pride would not let EWPR vanish.

Rumors indicated the minimum-security unit would go to Airway Heights, and soon afterward the Airway Heights City Council voted to accept both a work camp and a 1024-bed medium-security unit. Their vote got the attention of headquarters—Pine Lodge's closure was now a reality, though staff would have the opportunity to transfer to the new prison.

Rumors flew that Ernie Packebush was hard to work for, and talk also spread about me. Ernie had implemented the SRA, which had caused a lot of stress. It was easy to dish out blame. The rumors did not bode well for a smooth consolidation.

Pre-release construction was rapid. I spent a lot of time in Olympia. The task force studied Connell, Dayton, and Airway Heights because they each had sewer hookups. Bernie Warner headed the siting task force. He worked directly for Riveland.

Airway Heights was on a review list for the medium and minimum units, and Connell was on the minimum list. A group from Connell visited Pine Lodge. Shortly afterward, the City of Spokane, Spokane County, and the City of Airway Heights endorsed a new prison in their economic development effort.

* * *

In 1989 Joe Lehman was hired as secretary of Pennsylvania's Department of Corrections. His legacy in Washington was objective management, new prison standards, and formulaic staffing. Yet Joe left unfinished work and Chase sought someone to finish his projects. Jim Spalding seemed next in line to be director of prisons because he had worked closely with Lehman. I had not heard that Chase was going out of state.

Bob Enright retired after Lehman left. I hated to see him go, as he did good work. With all the talk of consolidation, I did not fill his slot.

I was in Olympia for an Airway Heights Corrections Center (AHCC) task force meeting and I met WSP Superintendent Larry Kincheloe for dinner. Larry told me he would be announced as the new director of prisons the next day.

I was surprised, but Larry did have military leadership qualities. He was also a fresh face. Chase would be comfortable working with Larry. It seemed a natural choice.

"Why tell me tonight?" I asked.

He and I were friendly, but not close.

"You worked at the penitentiary and you lived in Walla Walla," he said. "What are your thoughts?"

Larry was looking for a replacement for himself at the WSP.

"Would you like the penitentiary job?" he asked.

I thanked Larry for his offer, but Kathy and I felt Spokane fit our growing family.

If me taking the job was essential, I would have talked to Kathy. But in the 1970s, I and another Spokane staffer had been whistle-blowers for Prosecutor Don Brockett. If that information went public, it might be an issue.

"Tana Wood and Jim Blodgett are better candidates," I told him.

Larry thanked me and said he would look elsewhere.

The next day Chase introduced Larry as prison director. Days later, Larry hired Jim Blodgett as the WSP superintendent.

* * *

With Airway Heights as the likely site, I moved to the 1024-bed medium-security design committee to ensure a smooth transition from Pine Lodge. With Ernie's approval, we staged consolidation meetings. I answered staff questions but I would be leaving soon.

Design committee meetings were weekly two-day events starting in August 1989. I did staff interviews with Al Ramos, Tanya Marlton, Mary Smathers, George Bayer, and Mike McInnis and heard staffers' fears about the loss of Pine Lodge's culture. I advocated teamwork and worked on other issues in Olympia.

I met with Jim Spalding in design group sessions. Jim lived with Chase's selection of Larry Kincheloe. He walked Bud Inlet and the boardwalk to lose frustrations and pounds and to sort out his life. Some days I walked with Jim. He was baffled and frustrated.

Jim was too young to retire. It would be two years before he had enough state service.

I had a dilemma. I had told Kincheloe about Brockett and my whistle blowing, but I was wary that Jim did not know about it. Warden Rhay had hired Jim's father and uncle after politics had forced them out of Deer Lodge, Montana. Rhay had also given Jim a job, so he owed Rhay.

On one of Jim's visits to Spokane, I told him of my talk with Kincheloe. We were driving to Pine Lodge at the time and he went quiet. He did not ask me any questions, and I soon forgot about the talk.

* * *

With pre-release construction done, I moved from Walker Hall to the new administration building. My office was up front near Ernie's. Behind me was the business office.

In January 1991 I received a letter naming me superintendent of the new minimum-security unit at Airway Heights. At the time I was mostly in Olympia attending meetings, waiting for siting studies to end. Pine Lodge Pre-Release (PLPR) was born while I was in Olympia.

My first duty as superintendent was meeting with officials from Fairchild Air Force Base to extend sewer lines from Flint Road to Hayford Road.

Washington Water Power's economic development group had a presence in Connell and asked if Connell citizens could visit officials in Medical Lake. The Connell City Council wanted more data before finalizing its decision to accept a prison in Connell. The local leaders wanted to know the benefits and issues. Washington Water Power, seeking to increase power sales in Connell, was pushing the project.

I arranged a meeting between representatives from Connell and Medical Lake. In Connell, I answered questions from the city council and city manager. Soon after, Connell voted to accept the four-hundred-bed correctional camp.

Airway Heights Corrections Center 1991–1993

I pushed change during my eight years at Pine Lodge. Yet I was not at ease with the prison rituals of custody; I worked to manage the prison environment, stabilizing it so inmates could live in a fear-free environment. Absent fear, both staff and inmates could consider options based on their value, not based on fear.

I had left Geiger for PLCC with a why me mindset. I did not ready staff for the coming changes, but I left PLCC feeling that, one day at a time, staff had supported my effort.

I worked for a smooth transition at Airway Heights. I did not judge Ernie Packebush. He had realized more than I that Geiger was a new ball game. He better understood the impact of SRA on programs such as Geiger. In 1983, his vision had been proven accurate.

Spalding surprised me when he said he would support community corrections, as if I might not support consolidation. I had no issues with consolidation. My only interest was a smooth progression so there would be no overreaction from staff.

In 1990, Chaplain Al West had built a chapel at PLCC with donated materials and citizen and inmate volunteers. The chapel was the site of the PLCC decommissioning. Full-time staffers received a memorial plaque dated 1977–1991, for Pine Lodge's years of service. Jim Spalding thanked the staff for their hard work.

I also thanked the staff, but I knew that the Department of Corrections had abandoned diversion efforts in 1981 with its prison-building push. Probation was now a pathetic shadow of itself, but the DOC was still committed to building prisons. I feared that the oral history of probation was being lost.

I left PLCC feeling I had had an impact. My challenge at Airway Heights was to build a prison that allowed for inmate choice. I dismissed the issues of consolidation—we must and would cooperate.

* * *

I kept an office at EWPR, but I was never there. In spring 1991, Larry Kincheloe visited me in Spokane and took me to lunch at the Longhorn Café. Larry said he was moving to Alaska and he thanked me for my past support. Then he told me I would not be running the major Airway Heights Correction Center, in spite of the letter I had received in January. He gave no details except to say I might improve my chances if I took classes at the National Institute of Corrections in Denver, Colorado. He wished me good luck and I thanked him. I did not question him.

On the design task force were DOC staff and the architects of Zimmer-Gunsul-Frasca (ZGF). Janet Barbour, superintendent at Twin Rivers Corrections Center, chaired the meetings.

We started early and ended late as we drafted, studied, and adjusted the design. The schedule was tight, the sessions intense. At each meeting specialists arrived with input. I felt out of place as I listened to debates. ZGF had little history designing prisons, having only worked on the federal prison in Oregon.

I watched who invested in what and why. The loudest voices were security advocates, but security pushed costs up and made little sense because we were building a medium-security prison. Brick and mortar costs were the reality, and we were on a fast track—we had limited money and time, as political support could weaken at any point.

ZGF earned ten percent of total cost as their fee, so it was not easy to make cuts, yet we managed. One battleground for cuts was the number of towers. The general talk was to have four, but Chase and Spalding clashed—Jim wanted four towers, Chase none.

The result was one tower, and security fell to the back burner. Looking for potential savings, I looked for less controversial items. Initial plans called for three car hoists in the auto shop, at a total cost of $250,000. I had brochures and price lists that showed hoists in gas stations were installed for just $7,000. We saved $229,000 on that alone.

I proposed pre-engineered structures for support buildings. Jack Cornwell, chief architect of ZGF, seemed upset and I wondered if he would fight the idea.

At lunch Jack studied metal buildings at the Olympia Yacht Club on Bud Inlet. He returned to our meeting in favor of pre-engineered units, as he had seen functional design reflecting off the blue water.

Pre-engineered buildings saved money and made bidders more comfortable, as off-the-shelf buildings had easily estimable costs and used materials that were widely available.

Airway Heights would have both medium- and minimum-security units. I pushed to design a light medium facility that could not later be turned into a maximum facility. Historically, prison classification paradigms had shifted with bed needs. We could avoid that reality if we designed a truly light medium.

I tried to limit in-your-face security features and heavy-duty lock systems. Internal security would depend on visible staff and their ability to communicate, work programs, and strong unit teams. I frustrated hard-liners because I limited the ability to lock inmates down. But our perimeter fence was serious—double fences and stacked razor ribbon—because medium-security included some lifers.

* * *

With the design progressing, I shifted to a public works group, as a new law required that we find a general contractor construction manager (GCCM) to run construction. A GCCM guaranteed cost and quality and would build on time, on budget.

Our group was made up of staff from the Washington State Department of General Administration (GA), DOC Capital Programs, ZGF, and myself. We were the first project under this law, so we wrote rules as we went. GA chaired the sessions as we selected weighted factors to create a matrix for scoring candidates.

To apply, a GCCM must have previously built a $250 million project. The top five firms did value engineering, reducing cost while maintaining function.

In interviews we saw firms' work and asked each to squeeze dollars out of the project, as they were experts. It was fun to watch the project unfold. We selected a firm and started negotiating a final contract. Design work was still ongoing as the GCCM started value engineering work.

The firm selected was excellent, but tensions grew as we reached $8 million in savings. Five weeks into talks, the firm said our contract was not worth their reputation. Mouths dropped.

The firm said they, not GA, must control project funds. Chase Riveland came into our meeting and listened as the firm said we were ignoring the law. They thought GA was in control because they were the ones doling out dollars.

GA called the next firm and we started over, but ZGF had already updated construction drawings. DOC and ZGF did not see eye to eye on drawings, but I saw no concessions. Kitchell Construction arrived as the new GCCM, and ZGF had to eat the cost of previous drawings.

Kitchell found more savings, but delays by ZGF hurt everyone. Spokane winters would limit construction if shells were not built. Snow was not a problem, but pouring concrete in subzero weather was tricky. The delays created a legislative issue: questions would be raised if no dirt was moved before January's legislative session started.

To get moving, a decision was made to start work on the camp using prototype drawings that lacked final site elevations. The work would be done outside our GCCM—camp architect Johnson Partnership LLC oversaw these bid packages, not ZGF.

We did have $8 million in savings to offset the delays. Meetings with Kitchell were low key, as no one wanted another walkout. Sessions with Kitchell created $3 million more in savings. ZGF felt the pressure as their fee shrank with each change in drawings.

Issues arose as ZGF resisted changes. I was in Olympia weekly, so I was detached from local consolidation efforts. I heard reports but focused on the job at hand.

* * *

Packages for site preparation and the camp were granted. The site bid was more than we estimated, but the camp bid was $9 million lower.

Foundations rose quickly to beat the cold. Lydig Construction Inc. wanted crews working during the winter. Lydig panelized buildings so walls would go up quickly.

In January 1992 Kitchell moved into onsite trailers. My startup team moved in on January 6. The team was Al Ramos, Barb Enright, Mike McInnis, and Peggy Weatherman.

The challenge was to build a facility that focused on inmate safety but still allowed for choices, so I suggested changes in housing design. I suggested a bowtie footprint for the two-story open bay housing units, with 128 inmates per pod, 256 inmates total, with three staff providing direct supervision.

On graveyard, staff would drop to two as all outer doors were locked from central control. Lockdown would be from 9 p.m. until 6 a.m. Housing would have rear entry access for deliveries, detention, and maintenance. The rear areas would not be accessible to inmates, which would cut down on search delays.

Disorderly inmates would be removed without fanfare to cells in the rear. We would stop the practice of walking rowdy inmates through the population—no one would be made into a hero. Silent housing was the best housing.

* * *

Pre-release tensions grew, and there was talk of foot-dragging. I was gone, so it was no longer my concern.

Jim Spalding replaced Larry Kincheloe as prison director in 1991. I was glad Jim's patience had paid off.

I had not spoken to Chase, except to say hello, since 1986. I thought Chase wanted a superintendent with major prison experience. Perhaps Riveland knew I could retire and would not be a long-term selection.

In January 1992, I drafted a retirement letter to Jim. I would retire as of June 30, 1992, with thirty-two years of credit. With my letter in hand, I talked with Spalding.

Jim said to keep my letter and that I would compete for the superintendent job.

* * *

Kitchell's manager, Brad Gable, was in his forties with close-cut hair. He stood six feet five inches tall and had played center for the University of Montana basketball team. I was amazed as Brad entered or exited a car or plane—I could not believe he fit. He impressed me by giving his best day every day and wearing a smile.

His assistant, Rob, was a rock-kicker, a been there done that man from Flagstaff, Arizona. He had spent his life in this line of work. He was unpolished, which had cost Kitchell in the first bidding round because he did not seem professional in the interview.

Kitchell had staff with a get it done attitude. They were upbeat, as was Garco Construction Co., which won the bid for the pre-engineered buildings. They were impressive in their work. Bids continued to come in under estimate, growing our surplus as construction moved along.

Jack Cornwell, ZGF's lead architect, randomly appeared at weekly meetings. I learned that he collected Indian pottery, studied Indian tribes, and was aware of Indian wars fought at our site.

Jack Olsen was initially the program manager for the DOC but left early to work with GA on an Olympia capitol campus project. Jack may have foreseen trouble. Nancy Deakins, out of the military, replaced Jack. She ensured GA control and considered Bill Phillips, chief of GA design and construction, to be our leader.

Weeks into construction, Kitchell found flaws in the elevation specifications in a bid package. The foundations built by Lydig did not align with ZGF's elevations. They were off by a foot—to solve this problem one foot of dirt had to be removed from the entire site.

The berm on the north side had been planned. To save the cost of moving dirt, berms were added on the east, south, and west sides. The issue was resolved, but it was clear that Kitchell had no control over two packages: the site grading and also the camp build, which was won by Lydig. That cast a shadow. Lydig's history was to lowball bids and rely on change orders for profit, but Kitchell eliminated change orders.

We made front-page news during dirt removal. As the berms grew, the temporary power lines overhead were no longer high above trucks. One driver forgot his dump truck bed was up and hit a power line.

He jumped from his truck, which sat touching the line. In minutes, the truck smoked and got red hot. Then it was fully in flame, black smoke rising skyward. The charred hulk sat on the berm until insurance claims were settled.

* * *

My trips to Olympia ended as onsite meetings started in 1992. I saw GA push and the DOC pull to control work. Kitchell resisted their efforts but I sensed confusion.

Nancy Deakins was not present as verbal agreements occurred with handshakes. By law, Kitchell had final authority on the project, since they were the GCCM and therefore carried the risk. But Nancy sided with GA, which withheld and delayed payments.

Clerks from the DOC monitored work, and their okay was required before a check was issued.

With construction ongoing, AHCC staffers were busy. Barb Enright opened hiring. Others wrote policies and position post orders, selected bunks or furniture. It was a sidewalk superintendent's dream.

I had no escape incidents or program issues to report, but vague rumors said I was slowing down consolidation at PLPR. Gary Fleming was Olympia liaison for the PLCC/EWPR consolidation. He was Jim Spalding's man. As issues popped up, Jim's tone suggested that he agreed with the rumors.

Spalding limited my budget options for AHCC. We were on a credit card, as PLCC's allotment had stayed at EWPR and I did not get an allotment from headquarters. My purchase requests went to Olympia for approval.

I was not on Jim's wavelength. We did not talk of the future as we toured the construction. Yet he did not tell me to back off on giving construction input.

In 1992, Jim hired Andrea Bynum as command manager. She oversaw both Airway Heights and the Coyote Ridge Correction Center in Connell. Bynum was a large black woman who had been superintendent at a prison in Stillwater, Oklahoma.

She had a son playing football at Olympia High School and hoped he would earn a football scholarship at the University of Washington. I met her on the site one misty morning.

Andrea said she wanted to learn about Airway Heights and Spokane, to help decide if she would accept the superintendent job. She wanted a tour, so we walked the hundred-acre site through the mist. We had twenty-eight buildings under construction, yet most were just foundations.

The site was muddy and Bynum didn't have boots, so it was slow going. Midway into our tour she got tired but appeared impressed. She said she had issues with the spacing of buildings, so she would install internal fencing. I was silent.

I did not see Bynum again until the superintendent meeting in June 1992.

* * *

At summit meetings in Olympia, ZGF continued to seek payment for drawing changes. I did not attend the meetings, so I only saw half of the picture as construction surged. ZGF arrived back at Airway Heights without payment for the original drawings.

I heard less laughter after those summit meetings. Team members became less involved. Yet work continued, and good weather and another open winter helped total savings grow to $20 million.

That savings was Kitchell's cushion, but Chase Riveland returned $18 million to the legislature, which upset Kitchell. We were at the midpoint of construction in mid-1992, and there was still much that could go wrong as contractors and subcontractors picked up bid packages.

Bid openings were announced at the associated general contractor's office. On bid days, contractors and subcontractors sat on the edge of their chairs until a bid opened. Then the room emptied, and fifty chairs were reduced to four. Winners waited to qualify, learning of Kitchell's culture and methods, and talking about issues, discipline, and safety rules.

The process was a ritual. Big money was made or lost. Bids were contracts with duties and accountabilities; Kitchell resisted change orders once ink was on a contract.

The contractors had various work cultures, reflected by workers in meetings, reports, questions, and change orders. To watch them interact was worth a ticket. Some whined, others played games to get an advantage, and a third type was all business.

Kitchell ran the meetings, which were from 8 a.m. until 3 p.m., two days each week. In the meetings there was a crisis every hour as folks forgot that Kitchell was the GCCM. If I had an issue, I waited until after the meeting was over.

In the confusion, Kitchell withheld mechanical packages, and no bids were let. It was their insurance; failure to have full control was risky.

For example, two emergency generators from Sweden needed a voltage adaptation in a Pennsylvania shop.

The shop offered a slow work time at half the price of high-demand time, a savings worth half a million dollars. Kitchell sought savings and accepted the bid, but GA delayed payment. The units sat on a dock in New York, so the discount was lost.

DOC Capital Programs and GA earned their budgets by managing construction. Each received a percentage from the total cost in a fee-for-service arrangement, so the more money spent, the larger their fees.

I felt this practice needed review, as the public was paying the fees. Moreover, with a GCCM, both agencies were fifth wheels. But GA paid the bills on the AHCC project, so they set the rules.

Bad blood flared up, teamwork suffered, and trust eroded over slow payments. Despite these struggles, construction was ongoing through the winter.

* * *

The GCCM's pot was boiling, yet to onlookers it was smooth. I credited Gable for his focus. He treated me with respect even when it was clear that I had little influence. For example, initially I pushed for fiber optics but had no success. But one engineer misdesigned the communications vaults, which were too small to handle large lines. Fiber optics fixed the issue by virtue of being much smaller.

I was agreeable with contractors. When they asked to install plywood under wallboard to reduce future damage, I said yes. When they asked if power could arrive above ground, outside the security fences, I said yes.

Our main power source was above ground to our substation, but our emergency generators would allow us to run for days. Overhead power was not a problem.

When the design team asked what direction they should face the building entrance doors, I said that our winter winds were from the southwest.

* * *

Camp soon was complete as spring winds blew and the days lengthened.

You did not need to visit often to know where the name for Airway Heights came from, as a steady breeze blew constantly. Job applications filled our mailbags as the pace of work quickened. We began the staff selection process as furniture and equipment arrived.

I took long walks at noon. As I stopped smoking I gained weight, but the walks reduced stress and my waist. My walks were like Jim's Bud Inlet relief.

I got help from Brad Gable, who let us use the Kitchell warehouse for deliveries. We did not have final punt lists; until the DOC accepted the site it officially belonged to Kitchell.

Janet Glover was my budget liaison. She was helpful, but she held the budget close. Since she approved payments, I was not accountable. I did not press the issue.

We molded a culture while construction continued. I asked Al to visit prisons and learn what worked and why, so we could avoid mistakes. He returned with lists of potential issues. The reality was that most prisons were command and control units that created stress and friction, which wasted staff energy.

You do not find teamwork in cellblocks or breezeways. I sought to build teamwork at AHCC by using a variation of military boot camp in gateway sessions, which were sessions to attempt to develop teamwork and culture. The process used storming, norming, and forming to evolve common values. Storming meant everyone had a chance to give input on job conditions to the group. Norming was the process of everyone coming to a consensus. In forming the staff goes forward and live their decisions, and doing so reinforces the culture and creates teamwork.

In military service, basic training overpowers recruits and infuses each with a military paradigm in sixteen weeks. Military regiments sustained that paradigm with a code of conduct.

We could not do basic training, but we could spend time with new hires and do routine follow-ups to make staffers aware of our common vision and goals. Follow-up sessions trained staffers to mitigate conflicts, one aspect of a unit-team model.

To be effective, we had to simplify processes so staff could focus on governing. Simple, clear goals would empower staff and inmates. Staffers would need to articulate and then practice their beliefs daily in order to nurture team relationships.

As teamwork grew, that in turn evolved our code of conduct. Treat others as you wanted to be treated, speak truth, work together, and you were on the team. It was that simple—there were no complex formulas.

* * *

Spalding visited in mid-1992 and we walked the site, but there was no mention of future plans.

After the tour we visited Kay Walter at Geiger. I had not visited Geiger in years. I was surprised that Jim was interested in Geiger, but with both county and federal inmates, much had changed.

The main office was now outside the fence, and there was a new recreation and visitors building. After touring Geiger I returned to Airway Heights and Jim traveled to Connell.

Connell's 400-bed minimum unit was a twin of our camp, but Connell's builder, Walker Construction, had not panelized the buildings, so their build was slower. Walker was also facing labor issues because they were building in a rural area. Our pace was surreal as pre-engineered units changed our skyline almost daily. I submitted monthly status reports on construction and program startup.

Andrea Bynum's visits were dismissive. She once gave me a plastic box with a set of candy false teeth. I thought, "What the hell?" I found no humor in it. I did not ask for an explanation. I let it pass.

* * *

Life got thorny in August 1992 when a recruitment announcement was issued for the Airway Heights superintendent job. I felt the clock ticking, so I went full speed ahead.

I would run Airway Heights until replaced, so I brought in Pine Lodge staffers who wanted a transfer. We saw transfer requests from across the state but we hired local and kept local commitments. We saw a hundred applications for each position.

We cold-screened applicants' history and education, and that first contact with candidates was often our last. We notified each by letter; bad news went out quickly.

Those still under consideration interviewed with panels from major institutions. The panels scored candidates, creating ranked lists of qualified applicants.

We started at the top of those lists and worked down with background checks. If a candidate passed muster, we hired. We hoped folks felt treated fairly. We lived our goals and recruited minorities to ensure a strong pool. We hired based on merit—all our affirmative action hires were qualified, and we met affirmative action targets.

Andrea Bynum told me to hire only camp positions—no medium-security staff.

I felt Andrea was surprised at our success in minority hires. We benefited from Fairchild Air Force Base being nearby; there were many minorities stationed there who were interested in working at AHCC.

As the number of Spanish-speaking inmates increased, another goal was to fill jobs with Spanish-speaking staff to ensure we could communicate with our inmate population. Bilingual staffers earned a salary bonus of 5 percent for their language skills.

Staff transfers were difficult. All prospective transfers were qualified, and each had a reason for requesting the transfer, but we limited transfers to prevent importing cultures. We wanted a fresh culture at AHCC, not a good ol' boy one.

Gary Fleming monitored hiring and carried Jim Spalding's messages. He was likable, and put out fires in consolidation. Gary tried hard to act as if my interests were his concern, but I knew that even though he worked for Andrea, his loyalty was to Jim.

Gary suggested that I hire a particular person for a key job, but the candidate had a poor history. I told Gary that Spalding would have to order me to promote him. He was not a good candidate.

Jim said to promote the candidate, so I did. It turned out that hiring him solved a personnel problem at another prison.

* * *

Staff orientation classes were a gateway effort. We identified incoming attitudes in an effort to acknowledge differences. We asked staffers to express beliefs and listen for consensus, which eventually evolved into the Airway Heights way of behaving.

Security is reactive by its nature, and staffers in prisons with high-risk climates often resist change. Reactive attitude can cause denial and create stress. Con power exists in every prison, so it was essential that we talk about it. A prison investing in the status quo falls into denial, which can lead to assaults. Aggressive acts are a tool of con boss power. I felt change was good, not evil.

At the WSP, Bobby Rhay had taken on the con code his way for years, molding and managing it to his purposes. At AHCC we would create an environment with a staff presence, honesty, and attitude that empowered inmates to grow.

Our model gave inmates choice. Lacking safety, prison life turns into survival. I felt new hires saw merit in choice, but time would tell.

We asked managers to reinforce values concretely and follow agency rules. We validated performance in surveys and gathered input on program changes.

Our facilitators, Tanya Marlton and Laura Jense, led yearly groups at Pine Lodge. It was one thing to conceive the culture and another to create it. Marlton and Jense were key members who ensured that staff knew and understood that the classes were not a Heffernan thing. I was there but could be gone at any time, and I wanted the culture to live on.

I knew that once a rope was twisted it was hard to untwist. Thinking about my status wasn't useful because staffers did not have a vote in my future. I slowed general planning and stressed our need to first finish construction. We focused on camp operations.

The Washington State Corrections Officers Academy came on the site to train state and county staff. The academy staff liked that we emphasized values. They felt inmate presence was a touch of realism.

No one stopped me from installing limited choice. I often expected to hear a slow-down order, but instead I heard good reviews about Tanya and Laura. Olympia liked the team building.

* * *

Mature bureaucracies often produce complicated policies to supplant ethics, creating quantity rather than quality. A quality approach would emphasize shared vision, simple strategies, and a clear mission with fair rules that encouraged communication and options. A quantity approach only hides the fear factory for a time.

Although I lacked status, I pushed my vision. We only got one chance to start, and it was important to start right.

Jim preferred the status quo, not endless meetings about change. He brought only two initiatives to the table. First, he wanted to remove the requirement that superintendents have a college degree. We voted no.

Jim's second initiative was to set up a mentoring program for staff, and superintendents agreed with this.

In a summer meeting, Spalding announced that the Airway Heights job was open. I got looks. Jim later called me into his office and asked if I had any questions.

"I am an at-will hire," I told him. I had no issues. "Is my application wanted?"

Jim told me to submit it, but that my experience was an issue.

Although I had been superintendent at Pine Lodge for thirteen years, I knew PLCC was not as complex as AHCC and had a smaller budget by millions. AHCC would have two thousand inmates and six hundred employees.

* * *

Monitoring construction was low stress except for the sewer issue. With open trenches and pipes installed, I learned the mayor had not acquired easements. He had told me he had gotten signatures, but he had not.

By digging trenches we were technically trespassing, so we bought out the owners of the land. There was finger-pointing at me and a big waste of money for Kitchell, GA, and the DOC. I should have known.

In late summer 1992 the correctional industries board visited to look at the 80,000 sq. ft. Industries Building, a warehouse, and a building we called the food factory. The Garco buildings were impressive. Chase Riveland and Jim Spalding also attended, and I answered board members' questions. It was clear they had no rush beyond the food factory.

Inside the Industries Building was a massive, vacant space. I said it was best not to build out the space without specific plans because it would just cost money. ZGF was hoping for specific plans so they could complete their design work.

When Jim Blodgett was in charge there had been talk of moving the WSP's metal fabrication shop, but new boss Tana Wood wanted to keep the jobs in Walla Walla. There was space for a large bindery, private class-I industries space, or vocational programs.

I met with Boeing Plant Manager Philip Kelly about the traffic on Highway 2. My staff visited his staff about our plans and he gave us a tour. We talked of staggering our shifts to reduce traffic problems.

On tour, I saw that all utilities except floor drains were overhead. The ZGF design for the Industries Building at AHCC called for utilities in the floor. Kelly said the overhead utilities allowed for reconfiguration at limited cost because there was no need to tear up concrete slabs. Following his plan would simplify the Industries Building if all utilities were installed overhead.

I also suggested letting inmates pour the floors. Doing so would save money and the correctional industries board would keep flexibility on build-out. ZGF accepted the changes, and only drainpipes were installed in the floor. The pipes were laid on a grid in the main hallway, bathrooms, and classrooms using capital dollars and inmate labor.

* * *

Our draft manual was done as we hired and supplies arrived. The manual laid out guidelines and programs and established a ninety-day updating scheme to account for changes as we learned. Our manual was DOC boilerplate simplified. Staff had input on policies, post orders, and directives. We did not cut discipline, but we framed rules in positive language to avoid the mayhem of the 1970s penitentiary.

We opened the camp in October 1992 after the sewer was hooked up.

Once we received our occupancy certificate, chain buses arrived weekly with wide-eyed inmates. Work crews from pre-release brought jobs, so inmates worked and we ramped up smoothly.

I began attending fewer contractor sessions and asked Al to attend in my place.

* * *

AHCC's layout was medium-security, which was significantly different from maximum-security. Distance, not fencing, divided operations. Coded badges detected anyone who went out of bounds.

The majority of locks were street locks, and toilet fixtures were street standard. Prison hardware did not dominate waking hours. This method saved millions of dollars, as security toilets cost $1,200 per unit, but our fixtures cost just $35. Street keys cost less and were more flexible. The change in lock equipment was part of value engineering, as we improved efficiency by creating key zones.

Airway Heights did not have a big-house feel, but felt more like a college campus. If you had to be in prison, Airway Heights was where you would want to be. However, to stay, offenders had to follow rules, go to school, work, and show us they really wanted to stay.

My open model asked staff to mix, stay visible, and be effective contacts. Con bosses would fill vacuums with fear or muscle, so visible staff helped inmates feel safe. Safety was vital to maintaining control since the inmate to staff ratio favored inmates.

I was lucky to have staffers at Airway Heights who had opened Pine Lodge in 1978 and Geiger in 1979. They knew the drill: start simple and set limited goals. Let staff and inmates develop programs to address the population's real needs.

Programs rewarded good behavior, but did not grant license. Compliance was key—inmates improved their living conditions with positive behavior and choices.

We emphasized vocational training to give inmates goals. Classes were competency based and open entry and open exit up to mastery level. No one just took up a seat in class.

There were no dumb questions from staff, but answers needed to have a vision. If questions arose I wanted other staffers to answer them. This kept the staff engaged and improved staff education, because they learned best by teaching. Yearly core training was wasteful, a "cover your ass" policy to limit risks. That said we did test staff on key policies.

* * *

Construction meetings continued on the medium unit and our inmates worked the graveyard shift cleaning up and installing bunks and equipment. As inmates arrived they quickly adapted to the work and school requirements. Hispanics were surprised to hear staff speak Spanish.

Hispanic inmates at Coyote Ridge were near riot over misunderstandings and staff attitude. The majority of Connell custody staffers were from the Hill and had brought a maximum-security mindset to Coyote Ridge. No staffers spoke Spanish, so friction grew.

We sent fifteen Spanish speakers, led by CPM Al Ramos, to Connell to sort it out. Al transferred twenty-eight inmates. The uprising died, but the long-term solution, given their Hispanic population, was to hire Spanish-speaking staff as we had at Airway Heights.

In early fall the double perimeter fences with stacked razor ribbon blocked my shortcuts and walking paths. Contractors pushed to close up all the buildings before the cold winds came. We expected heavy snow in the coming winter.

The largest building housed medical, visiting, and reception, as well as the public entrance, administration, and master control. A public access area was partly outside and inside our perimeter fence, which abutted the two-story building.

The original plan called for tunnel access to the inside administration building, but basalt stopped that idea. Instead, the building had a security-barrel roof. It cost less and was a better alternative.

Construction issues were ongoing. One contractor built a wall poorly and it required a costly do-over. I said to use drywall for interior non-security walls, which saved time and money. I watched the drama play out. ZGF staffers looked glum, as they knew our cuts were not helping their bottom line. They said in the future they might work in the private sector, but for now it was time to finish and cut their losses.

With ongoing confusion over payments, Brad Gable was often in Olympia or Seattle. Senior Kitchell staffers from Phoenix visited Olympia. There were no bids left, and build-out was on schedule and still under budget.

The build affected the entire region. Lydig Construction and Garco Construction built most of the buildings at AHCC. Since they were both local companies, their work created an economic upturn in Spokane into the fall of 1992. The Airway Heights project brought city sewer and water to the west plains; it became a developer's dream, and a land rush of sorts started.

I seldom saw Bynum; I assumed she was not interested in Airway Heights.

* * *

Spalding told me that nine people applied for the Airway Heights superintendent post. Three other candidates and I received final interviews. I saw candidates with major prison experience as having an edge. I could accept that rationale.

A day before my trip to be interviewed, Spalding called. "An out-of-state candidate is going to visit," he said. "Can you give him a tour and brief him?"

What could I say but yes? It was a strange request to prep another candidate. Jim was testing my patience.

I gave a tour to the tall black man in his late thirties. The tour was positive—he liked the layout and obviously knew prisons. He did not ask me about my duties nor did I volunteer them. He asked how Airway Heights fit into the agency's plans.

"Washington needs medium beds," I said. "We fill that gap."

He talked as we walked. He was a quick study and seemed capable. I was impressed. Afterward I drove him to the airport to save him the taxi fare. I told Spalding the tour was completed, but I did not say that I was impressed with the candidate. Besides, I did not think he would be at Airway Heights for long; if he got the job, he would be in Olympia within two years.

With these thoughts, I slept well before my flight to Olympia. I lunched at Oyster House. My interview panel was Spalding, Blodgett, and Tom Rolfs. They knew my views. Interviews made me nervous, but I did not embarrass myself.

There were no questions about riots or major incidents. The questions were open-ended softballs. I could have talked all day. Yet I knew presentation counted as much as answers. If they were seeking a charismatic leader, one to influence large groups, I was not their man. I was a plodder. I covered my bases.

* * *

November was silent as I played the waiting game. People called and said they hoped I would get the job.

The gods smiled on our project—winter did not put snow on the ground. I walked the grounds daily knowing we would finish under budget.

Andrea Bynum visited and was dismissive. She felt nothing was happening with the medium-security unit. She told me to limit myself to camp decisions. I had heard it before and I felt it was stupid. Andrea had given me those candied false teeth and I had found no humor in the gift.

Finally I pushed back, asking if being black and female excluded her from being a bigot.

"Is 54 old?" I demanded.

She had no reply.

I said, "It is sad when a black woman discriminates."

Andrea left quietly.

Within a week she was apologizing. She said she had meant nothing by her gift; it had just been bad judgment. But I did not feel good about her visit. I felt she was covering her backside.

Come to Olympia 1992–1993

On Thursday, December 3, 1992, Jim Spalding called. "Be in Olympia Friday afternoon, December 11," he said. "Can you get a ticket?"

The waiting was over. I felt uneasy. Jim's voice was flat and there was no small talk. I flew Northwest Airlines into Sea-Tac.

I entered a darkened headquarters. "Staff must be out shopping," I thought. Dim lights were on in Jim's office. Margo Jense sat alone at her desk outside Jim's office. This did not feel right. Jim was at his table. He did not delay.

"You're not selected," he told me.

He thanked me for my prior work, but his tone was crisp. I wondered why he had called me to Olympia. I thought, "You could at least have traveled to Spokane."

Jim said, "Kay Walter has been selected."

"Whoa," I thought. It hit me like a ton of bricks.

I had nothing against Kay; I had known her for twenty years. She and Jay, her husband, had volunteered in the jail, and Kay had worked for the DSHS and later at Geiger.

But I was shocked. I thought, "Is he kidding?" Kay was a nice person and a hard worker, but she had less experience than I had. I had sat on her interview panel for supervisor. The experience excuse was crap and did not fly with me; this was not about my experience.

"Jim, why did you ask for my application?" I asked.

My thoughts were racing. It was nuts. What could I say?

I needed to walk and sort it out. The hardest person for me to manage was always me. I was angry but I didn't show it.

Olympia wanted me out so I would not be a fly in Kay's soup. I regained my composure and tossed my superintendent badge to Jim.

I shook my head. My career was over. The best I could do was to maximize my departure. They would pay to get me gone.

He said, "You keep your badge."

"No," I said. "I'm out of here. I will retire. I want to be paid for the extra time I worked on Pine Lodge and Airway Heights with a ninety-day home duty assignment as paid leave."

Jim had asked me to fly to Olympia on Friday. I thought, "He could have shown me respect and come to Spokane." I had worked for him for eight years. I had toured a candidate. He was a horse's ass!

I left that unsaid.

"Have a happy holiday," Jim Blodgett said from his office.

On the way to the airport I thought of my family. At home we would talk. I needed plans. Sea-Tac was busy with the seven o'clock rush. I was in a daze.

The personnel courses on discipline said to give out bad news on Friday. It would give the victim extra time to regroup.

"What would it have cost Jim to fly to Spokane?" I thought.

The hit took time to accept. Thankfully, I could retire and shake the dust from my sandals. It would not be the end of the world. My main task now was to put my life into context.

I owed Kathy more than I owed Jim or the DOC. I would not go forward looking back—it would be a fool's choice. This could easily have occurred in 1970 or in 1983.

My flight landed at nine and it was ten when I told my news to Kathy.

* * *

Kathy was more upset than I was. Kathy was my rock, a believer, but she knew I could not stay. I was three years beyond retirement credit. Life was unfair, but I was lucky—I had one heck of a run. My only option was to retire and move on.

"We can talk later," I said. I was tired. "I will sort it out tomorrow." I was asleep when my head hit the pillow. It was a deep sleep.

I woke when Kathy handed me the phone. It was a long-distance call from Canada. Frank's voice was clear. Years back,

Frank had called about attending his son's wedding in Yakima. Now he was calling me to say thank you.

His family was doing well, he said. I had had an impact.

Frank's call was a gift. I hung up and fell asleep again. Kathy confirmed the next day that Frank's call had not been a dream. Through Saturday and Sunday the clouds lifted; perhaps giving bad news on Friday really worked.

On Monday I told the staff that I would retire and Kay Walter would be superintendent effective January 19, 1993. People said nice things, though they did not change reality. I did not blame Kay—she was one of many who applied and she did not hire herself.

* * *

I met Kay for coffee at the Longhorn Café. We were only tables from where Kincheloe had said, "You will not be the Airway Heights superintendent."

I congratulated Kay and wished her well. She said she had known for weeks and that it had been hard to keep quiet. In that moment I felt that Jim Spalding lacked nerve. I thought, "How weak!"

I told Kay I would retire and she seemed relieved. It would have been difficult if I stayed.

* * *

It was December and soon the clock was ticking faster. Andrea arrived with my forms. I told her I expected pay for the extra hours spent on consolidation and the trips for Airway Heights design meetings.

I was leaving in January but my retirement would not be effective until March 31, 1993. She was confused, but I told her it was not her decision.

"You talk to Olympia," I told her. "I'll go find coffee."

In the end I was granted home assignment from January 24 to March 31, 1993.

* * *

Tom Rolfs visited in January before I left for home assignment to thank me for past help. His talk over lunch was confusing. He left me with a sense that Governor Mike Lowry had wanted a female for the superintendent position. Tom had not known that in June 1991, before Lowry was governor, Larry had said I would not get the job.

Jim Spalding visited on my last day to attend a coffee and cake gathering. He was doing good soldierly duty, but it was clear he wanted to be elsewhere.

He had supported me during my brother's troubles but we were not close. I was not an angler who felt a stream bank was happiness. Still, I was fortunate to leave. Jim stayed on after Kincheloe got the appointment as director of prisons and went through hell. I did not.

Jim thanked me for this and that. He did not look me in the eye.

I said, "I enjoyed working for you. Still, you had no class asking me to tour that candidate. You asked me to come to Olympia after knowing about Kay's selection for weeks. You have a good day."

What could he say? We shook hands and he crossed the lot to his car. Reality arrived as Ramos said the cake and coffee were ready.

We had a good turnout of visitors from downtown, the jail, Geiger, Pine Lodge, and Airway Heights. What could I say? Life moves on, thanks for the memories. Take risks, invest, and share a vision.

Airway Heights' culture would grow with or without me, as staff moved on. I felt lucky. I had gotten off the train. We all do in time.

I ate a piece of cake even though I disliked cake. I had punch and two cups of coffee. I stayed until shift change. It was midday, yet early shadows decorated a surreal world. A winter chill was in the air and a haze was growing. Large mast lights slowly pushed against rolling fog and cut through it. The whole area glowed.

* * *

The next day came to Lacrosse Avenue and I was up at 6 a.m. with nowhere to go. I took a month to grieve over my outrageous fortune. To take any more time would have been self-pity. I took walks and moved against the winter wind. I had mixed feelings, but the rough wind blew in my face and kept me in the present.

I got beyond bitterness quickly because it hurt only me. I have had challenges. The satisfying days were as a probation and parole officer and working in jail programs. Work release was not as much fun, yet I did like diversion. I saw no value in those WR re-entry programs.

Geiger, Pine Lodge, and Airway Heights were gifts. I had not planned the road; was it useful to open three units? It is too bad that today we do not use probation, as it is so much more effective than opening more prisons.

I had seen fear in prisons that went far beyond court-ordered punishment. I say let's not use fear factories if probation works.

* * *

Spring arrived with green growth. It was a time of wonder and I looked forward, not back. I remembered John Kennedy's "Ask not" words as a guide to giving and growing. They simplified life.

Shutting down was difficult, but retirement paid well. Our son Jason graduated from Gonzaga Prep and went to Carroll College in Helena, Montana.

I kept busy and tried to be useful, to express myself and use up energy. I decided that it may take time but I would try to write. Perhaps I could clear up the shadows of crime and punishment and the politics of justice in Washington.

I stopped at School District 81 for their volunteer options and was assigned to the Skill Center Advisory Board. I had held an interest in basic education since my days on the Catholic Diocese School Board and later on Spokane Community College boards.

Education changes people. The secret is to start where folks are. Teach to their interests.

An Irish Blessing

"May your neighbors respect you, trouble neglect you,
the angels protect you, and heaven accept you."